The Scots-Italians

JOE PIERI was born in Tuscany in 1919 but spent nearly all his life as a café proprietor in Glasgow. He writes for pleasure and is now retired. His previous books include *Tales of the Savoy, The Big Men, Isle of the Displaced* and (with Archie Morrison) *Wheel of Fortune*, also published by Mercat Press.

THE SCOTS-ITALIANS

Recollections
of an
Immigrant

Joe Pieri

mercatpress
www.mercatpress.com

First published in 2005 by Mercat Press Ltd
10 Coates Crescent, Edinburgh EH3 7AL
www.mercatpress.com

ISBN: 184183 0879 (paperback)
ISBN: 184183 0925 (hardback)

The publishers gratefully acknowledge the help of Ale Nardini in providing
the picture of the 1950s ice-cream van on the cover of the book and that of
the group in the Bar Capretz, Barga. His website, *www.scotsitalian.com*, is the
main source of information about Scots-Italian matters on the internet.

Set in Bembo with headings in New Baskerville at Mercat Press

Printed and bound in Great Britain by Bell & Bain Ltd

❧ Contents ❧

❈ Illustrations ❈

🏵 Prologue 🏵

In the writing of this book I have been able to draw on a lifetime of personal experience as an Italian immigrant who arrived in Scotland in the early part of the twentieth century, and whose life has mirrored that of many of the immigrants of those and subsequent times. I was brought to Glasgow by my father in 1919 when just one year old, and my memory is still vivid of those early days in what, to my parents, was a strange land peopled by persons whose language and customs were far removed from those of the Tuscany of their birth. They came away from the land where they were born and which had moulded their character and where they had lived all their life, in search of an opportunity to build a better future for themselves and for their two children.

My father Francesco had already taken such a step in 1910, when with his new wife Maria he had set out with hundreds of thousands of other Italians for the Shangri-La of the USA, where work was plentiful, it was said, where the pavements were edged in gold, where everyone was the equal of his neighbour, and where no-one had to touch cap obsequiously and cringe to authority in the search for work, or what in other more enlightened lands was considered to be the rights of a man. Until then, in the country of his birth he had lived the life of an unskilled 'bracciante', a labourer, one who works with his hands. Born in 1879 in the remote village of Cardoso high above Barga, in the last decades of the nineteenth century when still a boy he had tramped the streets of the cities of Northern Italy and of Southern France selling plaster statuettes; then as a teenager he had pushed a barrow along the streets of those same cities as an 'arrotino' or knife-grinder. In summer, at times he had worked the land in the hamlets in the hills above Barga, and there, in the farm known as Bacchionero, where he worked regularly at harvest times, he had met and married my mother.

Once in America, after the shock and bewilderment aroused by the sight of Ellis Island and the teeming overcrowded tenements of New York had been overcome, they found that life could be good, for if a man had a strong and willing back there was plenty of well-paid work available. A series of jobs in different places followed, and they finally settled in St Paul, Minnesota, where my older brother Ralph was born in 1912. Two years later, in the late summer of 1914, the First World War erupted in Europe. Italy did not enter on the side of the Allies until the beginning of 1915, for the simple reason that the Italian government of the day could not raise an army. Italy's manpower had been drastically depleted by the mass exodus of her young men in previous decades, so the government had to mount a wide-ranging recruitment campaign among Italians of military age in the USA, the country to which millions of Italians had emigrated. The Italian government offered these emigrants the earth to have them return and do military service. A lump sum on recruitment was offered, with free transport back to Italy for their families, generous payments on demob, and a guarantee of a house and work once the war had finished. It was not hard to persuade my father to return. My mother had been homesick since the day she had left her native Barga hills. Never mind that money was now being earned, that one did not have to barter for the necessities of life and that limitless opportunities beckoned. None of this compensated for the strange language and the different way of life in this distant land, and so my parents listened naively to the blandishments of the recruitment officers and returned to Italy.

As a soldier my father reached the rank of sergeant, and was lucky to escape the carnage of the battlefields of Caporetto and the Piave, but in early 1918 in the latter campaign he was hit on the temple by shrapnel, a wound which left him with a disfiguring scar by the side of his left eye. This earned him a discharge from the army, and he joined my mother in Bacchionero, where I was born three months after the end of the war. Disillusionment with the promises of the government soon set in. The old ways had not changed, the same corrupt and ossified social structure which my parents had sought to flee from still held sway in the country, the authorities did not live up to their promises and the poverty and social injustice from which my father had tried to escape and which the recruitment officers had promised would be banished from Italy, looked set to continue forever. Indeed, if anything, conditions were worse than before. There was little or no work to be had, and the chaotic politics of the day, with bitter quarrels raging between the differing groups of Monarchists, Bolsheviks and the newly-emerged *Fascisti* led by one Benito Mussolini, held out no hope of material progress. So once more my father's thoughts turned to the USA, but the way there was now barred.

Immediately after the war in 1919, faced with the prospect of a new and unwanted influx of immigrants from the poorer countries of southern Europe, the United States government had imposed a quota system of immigration which served to limit drastically the entry of Mediterranean peoples.

No matter that my father had lived and worked there for a number of years before the war or that my brother Ralph was American by birth; my father did not have the connections or the money to bribe corrupt officials and so he would have to take his place in the queue, which meant a wait of many, many years. Now that I had arrived on the scene, my father was faced with the bleak prospect of scratching a living in Bacchionero to feed not only himself, but a wife and two sons. With the door to America closed, he set about searching for another place where work was available and where effort would be rewarded. But where to go? And how to get there?

My father turned to the one agency which could offer help—the Church. The local priest, who came to say Mass in the little chapel in Bacchionero every Sunday for the benefit of the many crofters who lived in the neighbouring hills, was consulted. He was well-informed in these matters, and spoke of a city called Glasgow in the country of Scotland in the far north of Britain. A number of families from the district had found jobs there: a man from Barga named Primo Marchi had set up a string of fried fish shops in Glasgow and was looking for good and willing workers to man them. There were as yet no travel restrictions to that part of the world, so the decision was made, and with the promise of work and lodgings from this man Marchi, my father and mother packed their few belongings, wrapped us up to face the reported rigours of the Scottish weather and set off on the four-day journey to Glasgow.

Primo Marchi provided the family with a two-room tenement flat in Surrey Street on the fringes of the Gorbals to live in, and my father was put to work in one of Marchi's newly opened fish and chip shops, the Savoy, at the corner of Hope Street and Renfrew Street. There he learned to prepare and to serve a dish completely unknown in his native Barga, fried fish and chips, and although the working day was of 12 hours a day, six days a week, it was not as heavy and as concentrated as some of the work he had known in America. By the standards of the day his weekly wage of £3 was adequate, and each week a few shillings would be set aside towards the day when he would be able to set up a little shop of his own, for that was the dream of every Italian immigrant: a business of your own, a home of your own.

I remember very little about our time spent in Surrey Street. We lived there until 1925 or so, and the only memory I have is that of a constant red glow in the sky, day and night, which, as I was later to learn, came from the nearby iron works, Dixon's Blazes, where the blast furnaces were never extinguished. These furnaces were also the source of a fine red dust which constantly covered everything in the neighbourhood. I also remember the rumble and the puffing noises of trains as they passed over a railway bridge which almost touched the roof of the tenement and the soot which drifted down after they had passed. Driven by nostalgia, I motor through that district now from time to time. Surrey Street and Dixon's Blazes have long since been demolished, and in their place there is some open ground, but the railway bridge is still there.

After a few years, my father had scraped together enough money for the down payment on the lease of a little fish and chip shop of his own in Crown Street, and there, at about the age of five, my clear memories begin. We now lived in Crown Street above the shop, and I went to school at St Francis in Cumberland Street, where I soon began to learn that I was somehow different from the other boys there. I was a 'Tally', my parents spoke English with a broken accent, and when one of them came to pick me up at school I spoke to them in a language my school colleagues did not understand. For myself and my brother a strangely dichotomous way of life had begun. We were language-perfect in Glasgow English, so we merged well into the Scottish environment. But then after school hours our surroundings at home were of a purely Italian nature, where only Italian was spoken, so my brother and I grew up to be completely bilingual. Thinking back over the fifty and more years that they were part of my life, I don't think I ever spoke a single word in English to either of my parents. My brother and I could slip easily and effortlessly from one language to the other and from one set of cultural values to the other, and we were at all times aware of the difference in origin and way of life between ourselves, our school companions and our Scottish neighbours. To some extent this feeling of displacement, I suppose, could well have been created by ourselves. The vast cultural differences and the language barrier between Tuscan and Glaswegian made close contact with the locals impossible for our parents. For them socialising was limited to the occasional Sunday visit to one or other of the few Italian families in the neighbourhood, and my brother and I were never actively encouraged to introduce outsiders into the family circle. By the same token, I cannot remember ever having been invited into a local household as a boy.

I remember the Sundays in Crown Street clearly. On that day the shop did not open. Our mother dressed us up in our Sunday best, and marched the family off to Mass. Sometimes, on the Sundays when the Xaverian fathers organized special Masses for Italians, we were taken to the cathedral in Clyde Street to listen to the fire and brimstone sermons from the pulpit. I remember one priest vividly, Padre Calza, I think his name was. He had lost an arm during the war and used his remaining one to thrash the air and pound the pulpit as he warned us of the fate that awaited if we did not obey the commandments. He was a powerful orator, and on the Sundays when he said Mass there was not a seat to be had in the Cathedral. He led the singing of the hymns, and I can clearly bring to mind the high-pitched keening voices of the Italian women as they joined in.

Afterwards, our mother would have prepared a traditional Italian meal for the Sunday lunch. She was a marvellous cook, and Ralph and I would stuff ourselves with a pasta dish of some sort, served in a sauce that only an Italian housewife can make. This would be followed by a variety of roasts, and was rounded off with traditional Italian desserts. At this meal Ralph and I would be allowed a glass of wine, which our father poured with a flourish from a straw-covered flask, probably from Fazzi's delicatessen in Clyde Street. Ralph's glass was twice the size of mine, as befitted his greater years. Mother was an intensely religious woman, and after the Sunday meal the family was made to say the rosary together in thanks for all the blessings God had bestowed on us. In retrospect I don't think that my father was all that religious; he led the answers to the prayers at quite a speed, as if he wanted to get it over with so as to enjoy the rest of the day. In summer we took a penny ticket on the tram to Queen's Park at the top end of Victoria Road, to be followed by a walk in the park and then a stroll back home.

I also remember Sundays in Crown Street because of the singers who used to sing in the back yard of our tenement in the hope of having a penny thrown to them from one of the windows above. These singers all had loud, high-pitched nasal voices, and all sang the same songs. My mother never threw them money, but would always wrap up some food, 'a piece', and lower it down to them on a piece of string from our third-storey kitchen window. This method of delivery was resorted to after some dropped 'pieces' had burst open on impact with the ground.

On Saturdays there was no school, and on those mornings I helped in the shop preparing the fish and potatoes for the day's business. I hated that job despite the sixpenny bit I was given as pocket money at the end of it, for I always finished with some fish bones sticking out of frozen fingers. I remember the Saturdays too for the pitch-and-toss sessions which took place in our backyard. Ours was far bigger than the neighboring ones, so that was probably why it was chosen for that particular pastime. In a pitch-and-toss game a half crown or two shilling piece was placed on the ground and coins were tossed at them, the one nearest the target picking up all the money. These were rough and rowdy affairs which often ended in a fight, and the Police were always on hand to break the games up and arrest one or two of the troublemakers.

In the playground at St Francis, many a taunt of 'dirty wee Tally' had to be answered by scuffles and fist-fights, yet after school hours we would have to stand shoulder to shoulder with our tormentors from school in common cause against gangs of children from other schools in the same area. Those were the days when religion was much more polarised than it is now, and you had to be ready with some sort of answer when challenged by the cry, 'Are you a Billy or a Dan or an old Tin Can?' ('Are you a Protestant, a Catholic or a Jew?') and if the opposing gangs were bigger and stronger, woe betide you if you were not fleeter of foot. Those were the days of the infamous Glasgow gangs, of which the Gorbals had more than its fair share, and youngsters would model themselves on gangs with names like San Toy, the Billy Boys or the Cumbies, and roamed the streets in search of rival gangs to fight with. I was given strict orders not to mix with '*I loffari Scozzesi*' (Scottish good-for-nothings) and to come home straight from school, but it was impossible to avoid all contact with them, and many were the cuts and bruises tended to by a tearful mother who said the rosary daily and prayed that the family might find a better place to live. As I think about it now, though, the great majority of our neighbours and shop customers were decent hardworking people, who treated us with respect and kindness, and the behaviour of some in the district was as disturbing to them as it was to us.

When I was about 13 years of age disaster struck the family. My father took ill. Years of hard and unrelenting work had taken their toll, and he collapsed behind the shop counter during a busy Friday night session. The doctor was called in. I remember him vividly, the kind and gentle Dr Easterman, who routinely attended the family during the not uncommon bouts of measles, chickenpox and other childhood ailments. For his visits a lace doilly would be set on the kitchen table, on it a glass of vermouth with an amaretto or some such delicacy. Beside the glass some money would have been discreetly placed; five shillings or so, to be pocketed by the doctor with a polite cough and acknowledging nod before partaking of the refreshment. Dr Easterman carefully examined my father and prescribed a long rest in some place with clean air and wholesome food. As the one who as yet did not contribute anything to the maintenance of the family, it was my duty to accompany my father for a year's stay in Bacchionero, where he slowly recovered the health lost in the past years of strain, worry and hard work. I still had about a year's compulsory schooling left before I would have joined my brother behind the counter in the family shop, but schooling was not important to us. What was important was that the breadwinner recover his health, so as to take his proper place at the head of the family.

For a whole year I lived, worked and played amongst the magnificent chestnut trees of those valleys high above the town of Barga. With my two older cousins I helped to tend the sheep and milk the goats and the two cows which Bacchionero boasted of, and helped to thresh wheat with a primitive contraption consisting of two long pieces of wood joined by a leather strap and swung hard against the wheat stalks to separate the grains. Then I would watch as the grains were ground by a water-driven millstone at the neighbouring hamlet named Carletti and there I would help to load the landlord Bertacchi's half-share on to the mules of his agents. I still have clear memories of the small army of crofters and their families who came to Bacchionero at chestnut harvesting time, and I can still see them in my mind's eye afterwards, winding their way home to the valleys below, laden like beasts of burden with huge loads of chestnut flour, the payment for their labours.

I sometimes helped my cousins to char the logs of wood which would be sold to heat the houses of the rich people in Lucca many kilometers away. The wood was prepared by slowly baking the green freshly-cut logs over a slow fire, and to this day the smell of burning wood evokes in me the memories of those days. I once nearly killed myself by taking a ride on one of these bundles of charred wood which the *carbonari* (charcoal makers) sent to the valley below on a rickety funicular, and I clung on in terror as the load went whizzing down the cable until gravity brought it to a stop about a mile away and about 500 feet lower than the point of departure. For my foolhardiness I was given a sound thrashing by my father, a sure sign that he was rapidly recovering his health.

I enjoyed every minute of my stay in those hills, possibly because I knew that I did not have to live the rest of my life there and would eventually be going back to what had become my home. For, strangely enough, I had become as much an outsider in my place of birth as I was in Glasgow. There I was 'the wee Tally': here in Bacchionero and the surrounding hamlets I was '*Lo Scozzesino*', the wee Scots boy.

With my father now fully recovered, we returned to Crown Street in Glasgow. For a year my mother and my brother of barely 17 years of age had kept the family shop going and had earned enough to pay the rent and put a few shillings aside for the future. It is hard to visualize what life must have been like for them, a woman and a boy in his teens without the head of the family to fall back on; the hard unremitting drudgery of going to the fishmarket in the morning, the washing and cleaning of hundredweights of potatoes and several stones of fish, the preparations and the serving of the finished article to a clientele, a small percentage of whom were sometimes only too prone to address you with sneers and insults. It was during my time in Bacchionero that I came to realize what a culture shock it must have been for my mother to leave the clean air and simple life of her birthplace for the dark, soot-blackened tenements of the Gorbals.

Back in Glasgow, a series of other leased shops followed our shop in Crown Street, one in Butterbiggins Road near Queens Park, then one in Auchinleck, a mining town in Ayrshire. Each new lease meant a new home for the family and for me a move to a new school, which played havoc with my education. Around the year 1932, during our stay in Auchinleck, word came down to us that all the shops of Primo Marchi, the man who had originally brought my father to Scotland, were being put up for sale. The Savoy, my father's first place of employment, was offered to him, and he scraped up the £50 deposit to have the lease transferred to his name, with arrangements for the rest of the purchase price, £200, to be paid over a period of two years. The remainder of the lease in Auchinleck was sold for a few pounds, and the four of us, father, mother, my brother Ralph and my- self, set to work in the Savoy, a fish and chip shop that over the next 40 years was to become one of the best known of its kind in Glasgow, and which was to provide a good living for Ralph and myself and our respective families and which was also to serve as the foundation of future prosperity. We had to work hard, but that was no new thing for us; we had to put up with many a slight and insult and occasionally even physical abuse, but we were inured to all that, and the compensation was that our hard work was paying dividends. On my weekly day off I could jingle a few halfcrowns in my pocket and treat myself to a good seat in the pictures. Those were the early days of the talkies, and I would sit fascinated by the flow of dialogue from some of the classic films of the day: 'The Barretts of Wimpole Street', 'David Copperfield', 'A Tale of Two Cities', and suchlike films, the actors sometimes using words I was not acquainted with. So I would take note, bought myself a dictionary, and was soon able to command the vocabulary I might have had if my edu- cation had not been so circumscribed by events.

I was now nearly twenty-one years of age. Ralph had married, an Italian girl of course, for no son or daughter of an immigrant Italian family would even have dreamed of marrying anyone other than one of his or her own kind. Life had been good to the Pieri family over the past eight years or so, and the future seemed set fair to be even better, when suddenly, but not unexpectedly, disaster struck once again. It had been obvious for years that Europe was drifting inexorably towards another war. Mussolini and Hitler had come to power in their respective countries. Italy had invaded Ethiopia,

Spain was in the throes of a savage civil war between the forces of Fascism and its mirror-image, Communism, and Germany was making threatening noises to its neighbours in Europe. The little Italian community in Glasgow had been split by the war in Abyssinia. Some of the immigrants were favourable to Mussolini, some, including my father, whose great friend Bruno Sereni of Barga was fighting in the International Brigade in Spain against Franco, were not, and this divide came to a head when, on the imposition of economic sanctions on Italy by Britain, the Casa Del Fascio in Park Circus urged Italians to contribute gifts of any gold they might have to their motherland so as to counteract the effect of these sanctions. An agent of the Consul in Glasgow did the rounds of Italian families to ask for donations, and he was shown the door by my father with a barrage of invective against the Italian government and all it stood for. These arguments raged in all the places where the immigrants used to meet. Cooper's café in Howard Street, a favourite meeting place in the mornings for Italians after their visit to the fish market, threatened to bar them all unless the daily arguments amongst them ceased.

Then on 10 June 1940, disaster befell all of the Italian community in the UK. Mussolini declared war on Britain and we Italians immediately became enemy aliens. I have dealt at great length on this period in the body of the book and will not dwell on it here. I was sent to a camp in Canada, and after more than three years of imprisonment there returned to Glasgow to pick up the threads of my life. The family Savoy had been kept open during the war years by our now-aging parents, who somehow kept the shop going so that their two sons would have a place to work in after the war. In 1947, by which time Ralph had been demobbed from the Army and I had been given permission by the Home Office to take up business again, my brother and I started to rebuild our lives. One year later I met my future wife, Mary Cameron, and two years after that, in 1950, we were married.

In the book I have touched on the question of 'mixed' marriages by first and second generation Italians in Scotland. Nowadays, as can be seen from the columns of the *Giornale di Barga*, marriages between native Scots and those of Italian extraction are the order of the day, but 55 years ago such unions were frowned upon and actively discouraged by Italian families, and mine was no exception. Mother took to frantically saying the rosary daily to save me from perdition, and the rest of the family, with the exception of my father, who slapped me on the back and said I should marry whom I pleased, were equally opposed. It has to be said that Mary encountered similar problems with her relatives, some of whom thought it wrong that a Scots lassie should marry a 'Tally'. Eventually Mary was accepted unreservedly into the family, but for a time a certain awkwardness persisted when we mixed in our respective circle of friends. Mary died some eighteen months ago, and her passing has left a void in what remains of my life that can never be filled.

Eighty-five years have passed since I first came to Scotland. The Jesuits are reported as having stated that if you gave them a child to educate for seven years he would be a Jesuit for the rest of his life. I used to apply that dictum to my own formative years. I was born in Italy, and my family upbringing in Glasgow was that of an Italian child, the language I learned at my mother's knee was Italian, and to that extent I am Italian. Moreover, environmental factors throughout my life have never allowed me to forget that my name labelled me as a foreigner. But my education, sparse though it was, was Scottish, my wife was Scottish, many if not most of my friends were and are Scottish, and the country which has given me the chance to reach a certain degree of prosperity has been Scotland, and so to that extent I am Scottish.

The conditioning that one undergoes in childhood is never eradicated, the dichotomy instilled in me from my long-past Gorbals years persists, and I can easily bring to memory the taunts of 'dirty wee Tally', the fights in the school playground and in later years the taunts suffered when serving behind a shop counter. Although I often wish I had a patriotic flag to wave, I feel that I have none, and that perhaps I am that person of whom Sir Walter Scott wrote:

'Breathes there a man with soul so dead
Who never to himself has said,
This is my own, my native land.'

But then perhaps I am not, perhaps I have two native lands, with a chameleon-like personality which allows me to blend into either background, Scottish or Italian, when the occasion arises. The skirl of bagpipes, the sight of a mist-shrouded Highland landscape, the roar of Scottish football fans singing *Flower of Scotland*, the simple beauty of a Burns' poem set to music— all these things can stir my soul. And yet the same emotions can be aroused in me by the view from some Tuscan hilltop town, the scent of olive groves and vineyards, the poems of Dante and by the music of Italy, all of which go to make up the Italian part of me.

For I am probably neither one thing nor the other, but then again, I am quite possibly both. Perfectly at home among my Scottish friends and relations as I am, I can still be jolted apart by an innocent question which places me squarely into an Italian context. 'Are you going home to Italy for your holidays this year, Joe?'

And if I am in Italy, where I go frequently to visit my daughter Luisa who now lives there permanently, my friends and relations greet me with the friendly cry, *'È arrivato il vecchio Scozzese'* ('The old Scotsman has arrived').

🏵 1 🏵

The First Italians

I believe that it is probably true to say that the first persons to come from the Italian peninsula and make their way north as far as Scotland were those soldiers of the Roman legions who originated in the land we now call Italy. Not all Romans were Italian. Roman legionaries were recruited from all parts of the widely spread Roman Empire, and the ones who fought on Scottish soil and then garrisoned Rome's English outposts at the northern limits of their conquests would no doubt have included legionaries from Spain and Germany, with many also from Africa and the Middle East.

By 78 AD the Roman occupation of England was well established, and the general Julius Agricola had been appointed governor of Britannia, the name given to the island which had been conquered and colonised by the Romans. In 79 AD, the Emperor Vespasian, under whom Agricola had served, died, and Agricola was ordered by his successor, the emperor Titus, to continue north and to bring under the control of Rome the whole of the island of Britain. In the early summer of that year Agricola again advanced north, with the support of a Roman fleet, to a place which Tacitus, the Roman historian, calls 'Mons Graupius', and which some modern historians say was in what is now Aberdeenshire. The Roman fleet, heavily laden with troops and camp followers, anchored near the shore and the Romans spread inland to do battle with Calgacus, the leader of the Picts, who by this time had assembled an army of about 30,000 men, According to Tacitus, Agricola had two full legions under his command, together with 5,000 auxiliary infantry and 500 cavalry, and he estimates the full Roman army to have consisted of approximately 15,000 men. Although they were outnumbered two to one, superior Roman tactics and weapons routed the army of Calgacus, who, it is said, lost 10,000 dead for the loss of 360 Romans.

Despite this victory, the Romans were never able to subdue the warlike Picts, and their constant harassment of the Romans became a problem of such concern that in 117 AD the emperor Hadrian ordered that a fortified wall be built for the purpose of keeping the Scottish tribes at bay. Hadrian's Wall was to stretch from Newcastle in the east to Carlisle in the west, a distance of 70 miles. In 138 AD Antoninus Pius succeeded Hadrian as Emperor of Rome, and decided to build a wall further north to rival that of his predecessor, and this, the Antonine Wall, spans the narrowest point of central Scotland between the rivers Forth and Clyde. The remains of these structures stand as a monument to the fact that the Romans were not able to conquer and subdue the Scots, as they had done with the inhabitants of every other land they had chosen to invade and make part of their great empire.

During the many decades of the Roman invasion and occupation of different regions of Scotland, there must have been a great deal of intermingling between the Scottish population and the Romans. Every army on the march in those days carried with it large numbers of camp-followers, mainly women, who saw to the satisfaction of the sexual needs of the soldiers, together with servants and traders of all kinds who sought the protection of the soldiers in their travels. In ancient and medieval times there were sometimes as many camp-followers as there were soldiers when armies were on the march. There was a lot for these camp-followers to do. Pack animals had to be cared for, tents pitched, water carried, wood chopped, food bought or stolen from the locals and cooked. Then everything had to be packed up in preparation for the next march. During battles, the camp-followers stayed behind in the camp, often fortifying it and using whatever weapons they could lay their hands on to defend themselves against any enemy troops who might filter through the battle lines. After the battles, camp followers tended the injured, buried the dead and plundered the enemy corpses. These camp-followers played a part in the military campaigns of the victorious Roman armies, and most of them originated in the conquered lands. During the Roman campaigns in Scotland, many local inhabitants would have become camp-followers of the Romans, and there must have been many women of Pictish origin who gave birth to children fathered by the soldiers of these armies. Cassius Dio, a Roman historian who was later to become a senator, noted that 'not a few women and children' followed the marching columns of Agricola in his Scottish campaigns. It follows then that a significant number of Italian genes could well have gone to form part of the DNA pattern of some of the present-day inhabitants of Scotland.

The Roman occupation of Britannia lasted some 400 years, and with the decline and fall of the Roman Empire and the retreat of the legions the darkness of the largely unchronicled Middle Ages settled on the land. From pre-Elizabethan times we have references to merchants coming to England from Florence and Lombardy, but we have no way of telling if any of them ventured north into Scotland. In the days of Queen Elizabeth, a considerable number of Italians made their way to England: musicians, street entertainers, pedlars and merchants from the north of Italy, who were attempting to establish commercial ties with London, but it is not known if any of these travelled as far north as Scotland. Even the confidant of Mary Queen of Scots, David Rizzio, whose story is now part of Scottish history, did not come here of his own initiative, but as the personal servant of the Piedmontese ambassador to Scotland.

Centuries later, however, in the 1800s and 1900s, another wave of travellers from what had now become the newly established kingdom of Italy came to seek work and settle in the Britannia their forefathers had once conquered and colonised. A few elected to travel yet further, and came north to the Scottish lands the Romans had been unable to subdue. The ones who took the high road to Scotland were comparatively few, but relative to their numbers they began to make a notable impression on the country in which they had chosen to settle. From the trickle which started in the nineteenth century the number of Italians now in Scotland has grown considerably, to say the least of it. There are in the region of 35,000 persons of Italian extraction in Scotland, and of these the Italian consulate in Edinburgh lists approximately 7,500 as Italian nationals and bearers of Italian passports, 4,000 in Glasgow, 1,500 in Edinburgh and 1,000 each for Dundee and Aberdeen. There is not a village, town or city in the land where Italians have not set down roots and flourished. In the Glasgow phone directory alone there are 91 entries under the name Coia, a startling statistic in view of the fact that the Rome directory lists only nine!

These Italians came from various regions of Italy, from the extreme north of the country, Veneto and Lombardy, and from the far southern districts of Calabria and Sicily. Most of all however, the Italians in Scotland have their origin in two places, the little Tuscan hilltop town of Barga and its surrounding countryside in the province of Lucca, and the towns of Filignano and Piccinisco south of Rome. In the early part of the twentieth century scarcely a family could be found in these two areas which did not have a relative running either a fish and chip shop or an ice-cream parlour somewhere in Scotland. Few of those immigrants had a trade of any description, many had only a rudimentary education, none spoke English when they first arrived, but in a strange land with strange customs they adapted to their new environment and introduced services which had never existed before in the towns and cities of Scotland.

The well-appointed ice-cream shops that developed from the ice-cream barrows once pushed through the streets by these immigrants added a new dimension to the leisure life of the youth of Scotland, and provided them with a place to congregate and meet. Fish and chip shops matched the growth of the cafés and provided the working classes with a cheap and nourishing meal which grew to be a staple of their diet. Having established little shops of this kind, many of the immigrants sent for their families and relatives to join them and help in the modest business they had set up. Their shops were the precursors of today's glittering take-away fast food outlets, and of the Italian restaurants, pizzerias and coffee bars now to be found in every Scottish shopping centre and high street.

The history of the Italians in Scotland is a story of what can be achieved by people of lowly and underprivileged beginnings, with little or no education, and with nothing to rely on except their own inner strength and determination to survive and prosper, so as to provide for their families a future which they could not hope for in the land of their birth. It is also a story of how immigrants can enrich and bring a new dimension and flavour to the customs and culture of their adopted land.

2

The Scots in Italy

Lack of written records makes it impossible to hazard a guess as to the numbers of Italian migrants to Britain in the thousand years between the fifth and fifteenth centuries, although contemporary writings, scarce as they are, make mention of wandering groups of musicians and minstrels from the south, and it is likely that many of these could have come from the land we now know as Italy. Some research had been made into the music and songs played by these itinerant minstrels, and in the eighteenth century a Scotsman, James Oswald, a distinguished musician of the day and court composer to George III, made a further study of the music of this nature, which he believed to be Italian in origin. This music consists largely of madrigal-style pieces set to song, with repetitive musical themes such as are still popular in parts of Italy, where they go by the name of *Stornelli* or musical stories. Oswald published much of his work anonymously or under the *nom de plume* 'David Rizzio,' the use of the name of Mary, Queen of Scots' tragic court musician perhaps reflecting his own Scottish origins.

However, one way and another and certainly from 1350 to 1600, Scotland during this phase of its history was as much associated with Europe in general as it was with England. On the evidence from the records available to us, it can be said with certainty that in those centuries the number of Scots who went to the southern parts of Europe by far outweighed any who might have migrated north from those regions. Trade with all parts of Europe took root in Scotland and flourished; Scottish fashions in dress and architecture showed a greater French influence than an English one; Scottish soldier mercenaries fought in Italy and in every corner of the European continent, and for generations the kings of France recruited their bodyguards from among Scotsmen of good family. Scottish nobles and clan chieftains sent their sons to be educated in France and Italy. The sons of the Scots king, James IV, for example, were tutored in Italy in schools founded by Erasmus, the leading European educationalist of the time. Erasmus himself was educated at the university of Bologna, which was founded in 1088, and was an important centre of European intellectual life during the Middle Ages. Among those who studied at Bologna were Dante, Petrarch, Thomas À Becket, and Copernicus. One of the first and most long-lived universities in the western world, it was certainly the most renowned, and became the focus for the wealthy and powerful families of Scotland who wished their sons to have the best education available.

Moreover, one who was to leave a lasting impression on the history of Scotland had Italy as his birthplace. Charles Edward Stuart, called the Young Pretender or Bonnie Prince Charlie, was born in Rome in 1720. He was the grandson of the deposed King James II of England (James VII of Scotland) and the son of the 'Old Pretender', James Stuart, who had twice tried unsuccessfully to invade Scotland in order to seize the British throne. Charles Edward Stuart's mother was a Polish princess, Maria Clementina Sobieski, who also had been given an Italian education. Countless words have been written about Bonnie Prince Charlie, many songs have been sung about him and are still sung, legends have been woven around him and every Scot who has lived since knows of his attempt to restore the name of Stuart to the British throne. Stories are told of his battles against the English, of his eventual defeat at Culloden, and of the heroine Flora MacDonald who helped him escape from his enemies and of his return to Rome where he died in 1788. In St Peter's basilica in Rome, directly over the crypt where the bodies lie buried, there stands a monument to the Stuart kings. The inscription reads:

> *To James III,*
> *son of James II, King of Great Britain,*
> *to Charles Edward,*
> *and to Henry, Dean of the Cardinal Fathers,*
> *sons of James III*
> *the last of the Royal House of Stuart*

Italian archives relating to the thirteenth and fourteenth centuries carry an abundance of references to the travels and exploits of Scottish soldiers who made their living in the service of Italian city states during that epoch. These were the much sought after Scottish soldier mercenaries who sold their services to the person who paid them most, or to the leader they thought most worthy of serving in battle. Those were the years when the Middle Ages were coming to a rapid close, when the dawn of the Renaissance was spreading throughout Europe and the Italian peninsula had divided itself into scores of small city states. Each of these tiny principalities had its own rulers, who fought constantly to overthrow or to kill one another for land, wealth and power. Their size and lack of manpower meant that none of these principalities had enough subjects of military age to be able to form armies of any size or worth, but they did have an abundant supply of money, for Italy and its city states at that time through trade had become one of the richest lands in Europe. The lords and rulers of these city-states realized that the only way to protect themselves and their tiny kingdoms was to use some of their vast wealth to hire mercenaries, or free soldiers.

The leaders of these mercenaries, whatever their nationality, were known as '*condottieri*', and fought for the most part for money and not for patriotism or glory. To survive and to be successful in their trade the *condottieri* had to possess a mixture of military ability and business acumen, and had to be able to negotiate suitable terms with a prospective employer. They had to be capable of judging the military strength and monetary worth of those who offered to hire them, especially the former, for they had no wish to ally themselves to a hopeless cause. In an age where disease and hardship took their toll of the young and where the iron workers who could fashion good and reliable weapons were scarce, the *condottieri* were reluctant to waste good fighting men and expensive equipment, both of which were commodities hard to come by. For this reason a campaign usually saw more tactical manoeuverings and military posturings than battles, and was very often settled through negotiation before much blood had been spilled.

As far as the person who hired them was concerned, the employment of mercenaries was a step to be very carefully considered, because these hired soldiers were not to be completely trusted. It had not been unknown for them to change allegiance when somebody on the opposing side showed them enough gold. Moreover, it was also not unknown for a successful and powerful mercenary captain to attempt the overthrow of his employer and seize his lands and castles for himself. All these negative factors did not apply to Scottish mercenaries, for they had over the years acquired the reputation of being fierce fighters and completely loyal to the leader who had paid for their services. This reputation was one they shared with the Swiss, and fortunate indeed was the city-state which could hire such soldiers to help them in their constant battles with rival cities. A contemporary writer, Vasari, gives this description of the Scottish warriors:

> 'Their aspect is terrifying. They are very tall in stature, much
> taller than most men, with rippling muscles under clear white

skin. Their hair is blond, but not naturally so. They bleach it artificially, washing it in lye and combing it back from their foreheads. They look like wood demons, their hair thick and shaggy like a horse's mane. Some of them are clean shaven, but others, especially those of high rank, shave their cheeks but leave a moustache that covers the whole mouth and which when they eat and drink acts like a sieve, trapping particles of food. The way they dress is astonishing; they wear brightly coloured and embroidered shirts, with trousers known as trews and cloaks fastened to the shoulders with a brooch, the cloak heavy in winter and light in summer. These cloaks are striped or chequered in design, with the separate checks close together and in various colours.'

The historian Pietro Egidi describes them as follows:

'These Scottish soldiers were very well armed, with bow and arrow and broadsword of the best quality. Some had horses, but mostly went on foot. They were well trained and skilled in the arts of war and no better archers were to be found. Many mercenaries from other countries were undisciplined, seeking only plunder and rape, but the Scots took pride in their prowess and had the reputation of being brave and loyal and faced up to any risk in battle. They spilled their blood almost everywhere on the Italian peninsula, in Lombardy, in Umbria, in the Abruzzi and in the Romagna.'

Scottish mercenaries at the end of the thirteenth and at the beginning of the fourteenth century probably came, in the main, from the defeated army of William Wallace at the battle of Falkirk, where on 22 July 1298, Edward I at the head of England's 90,000-strong army attacked a much smaller Scottish force led by Wallace. The English army had not only a numerical advantage over the Scots, but was also infinitely better equipped. It had the fearsome longbow at its disposal, and the English archers decimated Wallace's spearmen and cavalry by firing scores of arrows over great distances, against which Wallace's men had little defence. The estimated number of the Scottish slain was between 8,000 and 10,000 men and the remnants of Wallace's army were dispersed. Some of these soldiers continued to serve their leader until his final capture by the English enemy, but many simply vanished from sight, and it was some years later at the battles of Cortenova and of Pavia in the early part of the fourteenth century that the first mention of Scottish soldier mercenaries is made in Italian historical archives. In those battles, where the king of France, Francis I, was defeated and captured by the Spanish at the beginning of their conquest of Lombardy, about 500 Scottish mercenaries were engaged in fighting for the winning side and probably as many for the losing one, for it could often happen that different bands of mercenaries of the same nationality would hire themselves out to opposing factions. They did not care whom they fought against, as long as they were paid for doing so. Every year, to commemorate the Battle of Cortenova, and the defeat of the French, a feast day is held in that town by the city fathers, and mock battles are staged with medieval weapons in the costume of the day, many of which bear a startling resemblance to well-known Scottish tartans. Bagpipes are played, and the tunes they play would not be out of place in a gathering of clans in a Scottish glen.

One of the most remarkable remains of the Scottish mercenary presence in Italy is the little town of Gurro, a few miles north west of Lake Maggiore in the Italian Alps. After the disastrous defeat of the French army at the battle of Pavia in 1525 by the Spanish, the hundreds of Scottish mercenaries in the service of Francis I of France, who by reason of their superior discipline had managed to escape the near-annihilation of the French army, sought refuge in the neighbouring wild alpine countryside. The defeated Scots set off in the direction of Germany, where they probably hoped to sell their services to some other prince. Instead, they came across the little hamlet of Gurro, a secluded cluster of buildings in a remote valley which reminded them of their native Scottish glens, and there they remained. According to legend, they were welcomed with open arms by the women of the village, who had lost all their young men in the wars. The people of Gurro, now a picturesque mountain town of a few thousand inhabitants, are in the main tall and fair with blue eyes and have a Scottish look about them. The inhabitants of surrounding villages refer to Gurro as 'La terra degli Scozzesi' (The land of the Scots), and the local dialect, a mixture of French, Milanese and German, contains hundreds of Gaelic words.

The local museum, which forms part of the the town church, contains such relics as the tartan material worn in the town until the eighteenth century and an assortment of belt and harness buckles and rusty weapons belonging to the original Scottish settlers. In the museum there is also a copy of a book written by Lieutenant Colonel Gayre of Gayre and Nigg, *The Lost Scottish Clan of Gurro Navarra*, in which he chronicles the history of Gurro and of the Scottish soldiers who settled there. These relics were the inspiration for the pattern of a new Scottish-Italian tartan which will shortly be unveiled. The design, the brainchild of Mr Cirignaco, the owner of the Bothwell Bridge Hotel, and Mr Davidson, the owner of a weaving mill, is a red, green, white and blue pattern of squares which has been patented pending the first weave at the Davidson mill in Glencairn. Although no official register of Scottish tartans exists in law, the new Scots-Italian tartan is to be submitted to the Scottish Tartan Society for recording in their list of tartans. The new Scots-Italian tartan has not met with unqualified approval, however. Giuseppe Zaccagnino, the Italian consul in Edinburgh, when interviewed on the matter, did not think it was a good idea and remarked that tartan cloth is everywhere associated with Scotland. What would be the reaction in Italy, he asked, if someone from Scotland were to attempt to introduce a Scottish pizza there?

A regular employer of Scottish fighting men was the famous *condottiere* Sir John Hawkswood, the English mercenary who came to Italy around the middle of the fourteenth century, after serving with Edward III in the French wars. Before he embarked on his French campaigns, Hawkswood had earned a knighthood in England, and after some years of fighting on French soil for whoever paid him most, he left that country for Italy, where he hired his services to a band of English mercenaries known as the White Company. His prowess with all types of weapon, his knowledge of military tactics and his bravery in battle had him quickly moving up the ranks until he became the leader of the White Company, a title he held for 30 years. John Hawkswood, whose band of mercenaries contained a good number of Scots, some of whom bore the name 'McCrimmon', was given the name '*Giovanni Acuto*' by the Italian states who vied with one another for the use of his services. He served the rulers of Pisa against the might of Florence, then fought against the Visconti of Milan, and on occasion sold the services of his White Company to the Vatican, which was then under the rule of Pope Gregory XI. In a move characteristic of the dedicated mercenary who fights for who pays the most, he finished his career in the service of the Medicis of Florence, whom he had fought against not so many years before by the side of the rulers of Pisa. For switching allegiance to the Medici family, who were in the process of making Florence one of the most powerful cities in all of Italy, he was paid 130,000 ducats in gold and was given a magnificent state funeral when he died in that city. He lies buried in the church of Santa Maria Novella in Florence, where an equestrian monumental fresco by Paolo Uccello marks the site of his tomb.

There are some historians who attempt to make a connection between the McCrimmons who served in Hawkswood's White Company and the city of Cremona in the north of Italy. There is no doubt that Scottish mercenaries were active for decades in northern Italy, and in an attempt to link the clan McCrimmon with the Cremona region in Lombardy they cite the fact that the name McCrimmon was originally 'Cremonach' in the Gaelic and that many of the inhabitants of the Cremona region are tall, fair and blue eyed. They also point to the fact that in the same region the use of bagpipes, which are very similar to the modern Scottish instruments, dates back to the late middle ages. It is also pointed out that Alba, the name of a town in Northern Italy where Scottish mercenaries were active, is the Gaelic word for Scotland, and there are some members of the clan McCrimmon who to this day hold firmly to the belief that the roots of their clan go back to those mercenary days in Italy.

The popes of the day made much use of mercenaries. The papal state, rich in money and belongings, paid them well, often far outbidding enemy states for the services of these professional soldiers. The popes who hired them were quick to note that the most reliable of the mercenaries were the Swiss and the Scots, and in 1505 Pope Julius II decided to form a personal guard made up of these professional soldiers who stood aloof from the political rivalries and treacheries that were the way of life in the Italy of Renaissance times. The Swiss were chosen in preference to the Scots, because, again according to the historian Egidi: 'They were more orderly in their appearance, less prone to argue amongst themselves and with their superiors, and more observant of their religious duties.' Another factor which told against the Scottish mercenaries was the fact that they had no undisputed homeland where recruits could be enlisted. The Swiss Guards have guarded the popes and the papal palaces to this day.

In the year 1561 an obscure Italian poet-musician made a fateful trip to Scotland, a journey which was to end with his burial in the Canongate Kirkyard in Edinburgh in 1566. David Rizzio was born in the town of Pancaglieri near Turin in 1533, the son of a well-known musician. He was a gifted child, and by the age of twenty he too had become a versatile musician and fluent in several languages. He went into the service of the royal house of Savoy, becoming the personal secretary to a Piedmontese diplomat, and travelled with him to his various postings in the capital cities of the continent. His employer was appointed to Scotland as ambassador, and took up residence in Edinburgh. There Rizzio met Mary, Queen of Scots, and after a few months the ambassador was persuaded by the Queen to release Rizzio into her service. There are sources which say that the Queen had already known Rizzio in France, where he had lived for some time in the service of the same ambassador.

Queen Mary was born on 8 December 1452 as Mary Stuart, and was the only child of King James V of Scotland and his French wife, Mary of Guise. On the death of her father, at the age of five, Mary was taken by her mother to France to be educated. There she was brought up at the court of King Henry II and his queen Catherine, where she spent a childhood of spoiled luxury. Mary's education was as broad as access to the best tutors of the day could make it, and in addition to English she was taught Latin, Italian, Spanish, and some Greek. French now became her first language, and indeed in every other way Mary grew up as a Frenchwoman rather than a Scot. In April 1558 she was married to Francis, eldest son of Henry and Catherine. The accession of Elizabeth Tudor to the throne of England in the same year meant that Mary was, by virtue of her Tudor blood, next in line to the English throne. Those Catholics who considered Elizabeth illegitimate because they regarded Henry VIII's divorce from Catherine of Aragon and his marriage to Anne Boleyn as invalid, looked upon Mary as the lawful queen, and Mary's father-in-law, Henry II of France, actually claimed the English throne on her behalf. The death of Henry in 1559 brought her husband Francis to the French throne and made Mary queen consort of France, until Francis' premature death in December 1560 made her a widow at the age of 18. Following the death of her husband, Mary returned to Scotland and in July 1565 married Lord Darnley, a Scottish nobleman, and soon after gave birth to a son, James. The couple became estranged shortly after James was born, and Mary began to take more than a passing interest in David Rizzio, who by now had become her private secretary and close adviser. She took to inviting him to her private chamber at night where they would work for hours together, and where Rizzio would entertain Mary with his lute and his songs. They would occasionally spend hours playing chess together, all of which gave rise to the whispered gossip that they had become lovers. Darnley became insanely jealous, and on 9 March 1566, armed followers of Darnley broke into the private chamber where she and Rizzio were, and hacked him to death with daggers. His body was thrown into the courtyard of the castle, where it lay for a time, and from there it was subsequently buried in the Canongate cemetery.

❄ 3 ❄

The Orkneys

I consider it to be a strange and remarkable historical coincidence that two events separated by six centuries should link Scotland and Italy together, and that the place where these happenings took place should have been at one of the most northern and inaccessible parts of Scotland, a part of the country least likely ever to have connections with anybody from the Italian peninsula far to the south. The first of these events took place in the Orkneys at the end of the fourteenth century, and the second 600 years later in the same islands during the Second World War in the years 1941 to 1945.

There are many conflicting historical writings about the first of these events and an encrustation of myth and legend has been shaped around the story of the Zeno brothers and their patron, Lord Sinclair of the Orkneys. With the passing of centuries the truth of these happenings has been lost in the mists of time, but what follows is a distillation of the many writings which tell of events that took place in the year 1390 in the Orkneys and in the lands and seas further west.

In that year, two Venetian brothers set sail from Venice in search of their own particular El Dorado. The two were Nicolo and Antonio Zeno, Venetian navigators and explorers who had come into possession of a strange and unbelievable map, a map which, according to them, had been given to an ancestor who had fought with the Knights Templar in the Crusades in the Holy Land. Nothing is known, nor is there any speculation as to how this strange map which charted a remote part of northern Europe and places west of that could have come into the hands of crusading knights. Be that as it may, the map did exist, bore the title 'The Map of the North', and charted the seas at the far north of the British Isles, where the location of a large island named '*La Terra Verde*' (Greenland) was indicated. *La Terra Verde* was shown on the Zeno map as being west of the Orkney Islands in the far north of Scotland. The Orkney islands were known to the Romans, who called them *Orcades Insulae*, and are mentioned by Pliny and Tacitus as having been

24

discovered by the scouts of Julius Agricola who had the coast of Britannia explored by his ships of war in 69 AD.

The two brothers set out from Venice in search of this mysterious Green Land and set sail across the width of the Mediterranean, through the straits of Gibraltar, then north through the Bay of Biscay, skirted the coast of England, navigated along the west coast of Ireland and still further north until they arrived in the vicinity of the Orkney islands, at the extreme north of the British Isles, all of which in itself was a remarkable feat, given the lack of accurate navigational instruments available in those times. Following the instructions on their mysterious map the Zeno brothers then turned west in search of their *Terra Verde*. When only a few miles west of the Orkneys a violent storm arose and drove them ashore on one of the islands of the group, which from the description in the Zeno narrative was probably the island of Burray. At the end of the fourteenth century the Orkney islands, which had been under the control of Magnus the Norwegian, had been ceded by him to King Alexander II of Scotland in return for a yearly tribute. Alexander in turn had entrusted them to the stewardship of a Scottish nobleman, Lord Sinclair, who also held the title of Prince Henry Sinclair. Lord Sinclair, hearing of the shipwreck and of the nature of the crew, went to investigate. He gave shelter to the crew, and was delighted to learn the identity of the commanders. The name Zeno was well known to him, for there was a third brother in the Zeno family, Carlo, an admiral in the Venetian navy, whose exploits were well known to Lord Sinclair. It had always been Lord Sinclair's ambition to dominate the northern seas in the vicinity of the Orkneys, and he reasoned that with the help of the two shipwrecked Venetians he could bring that ambition to fruition. He immediately appointed Nicolo, the elder of the two, as commander of the Sinclair fleet. A cannon was salvaged from the wrecked Venetian craft and Sinclair was shown how this could be mounted on board one of his ships and pivoted to target the enemy without manouvering the craft.

Lord Sinclair was also a grand master of the Knights Templar and a veteran of the Crusades, and he listened with enthusiasm to the Zeno brothers as they told of their map and of their ambition to find *La Terra Verde* and its treasures. He was convinced of the authenticity of the map, and gathered a fleet of twelve ships to sail west under the command of the Zeno brothers. The fleet left the Orkneys in 1392, and according to writings of the elder Zeno brother, having rested for a while in Greenland, Lord Sinclair's fleet sailed further west and landed in what is now Nova Scotia, where they wintered prior to exploring the eastern seaboard of the United States. As military adviser, Henry Sinclair brought with him a Scottish Highland knight, Sir James Gunn, who took ill and died during this exploration. As far as can be determined from the Zeno map and from manuscripts preserved in Venice, Gunn's death took place in an area near to the bay where Boston harbour now stands. Carved on a rock face in Westford, Massachusetts, there is a mysterious effigy which could well be the representation of a soldier in the type of body armour worn by the knights of the late middle ages. The image shows an armoured head, a shield and a fourteenth century broadsword and pommel. The heraldic emblems on the shield have been identified as being those of the Gunn clan of northern Scotland, vassals of Lord Sinclair. When first discovered by modern archaeologists it was thought that the carving was the work of indigenous Indians, but this theory was later discarded, since the tools available to the natives could not have chiselled into the hard rock where the effigy stands, nor could they have had any knowledge of heraldic emblems or body armour of that day.

The Micmac Indian tribe of Nova Scotia have a legend which speaks of a king and two brothers who came with many ships from an island far across the sea. They are said to have landed on the shore near the tribe's village with many soldiers, stayed for a year and then departed, leaving behind one of their ships which had been sunk in a storm. In 1850 a cannon was dredged from the harbour of Louisberg on Cape Breton island, and it was identified as being a naval cannon of fourteenth century Venetian design. The cannon is exhibited in the museum of that town.

The Zeno narrative and map of the voyage of Lord Sinclair, which was later published in Venice, records that the explorers sailed down the coast to what is now the town of Westford, Massachusetts, and discovered what is now known as the Merrimack River. They explored inland until they came upon a small tributary known to the Indians as the Stony River, where they made anchorage just a short distance from the present-day Westford. Several large engraved mooring stones have been found along the banks of the river indicating that as many as twelve long boats could have been tied up here. Prince Henry and his fleet returned to the Orkneys, and shortly after his return he died there, some say by assassination.

The Zeno brothers returned to their native Venice with a record of the voyage, together with their famous Zeno Map, amended by them to include details of the journey they had just undertaken. Not only did the new Zeno Map chart the sea with remarkable precision, it also showed certain land-marks which exist to this day. For example, it illustrated two inhabited cen-tres in Estotilanda (Nova Scotia), where Louisburg and St Peter's now stand,

and marks out a little island which they called 'Isola della quercia' (Oak Island). The brothers' story was greeted with disbelief in Venice, where some of the Doges of the city refused to believe that there was such a place as the Orkney Islands, despite the fact that it had been charted by the Romans, let alone a land much further west. Copies of the map and the narrative were circulated to centres of learning in Italy and were much discussed in the university of Bologna, where arguments raged as to its authenticity. The original Zeno map and narrative describing the voyage were kept in the family, and in 1558, a descendant, also named Niccolo, made a printed book from the original manuscript. The Zeno brothers had returned to Venice in the year 1400, and it was another 92 years before Cristobal Colon, better known to us as Columbus, made his historic crossing of the Atlantic. He must have been acquainted with the Zeno narratives, since he too had studied for some time at the University of Bologna.

Off the coast of Nova Scotia there is a small piece of land known as Oak Island, so named because it is the only place within hundreds of miles where the oak tree grows. One summer day in 1795 a young man, Daniel McGinnis, came across a curious circular depression in the ground. Standing over this depression was a tree whose branches had been cut in a such a way as to suggest it had been used as a pulley. McGinnis went home to get friends and digging equipment and returned later to investigate the hole. They made an amazing discovery. Two feet below the surface they came across a layer of flagstones covering the pit. At 10 feet down they ran into a layer of oak logs spanning the pit. Again at 20 feet and 30 feet they found the same artefact at intervals of ten feet, a layer of logs, some covered with charcoal, some with fibre. Over the years and into modern times digging has continued at the site sporadically. A depth of 90 feet has been reached, and the incredible and undisputable fact is that at ten foot intervals a layer of oak logs is found, some with fibre and some with charcoal coverings. At 90 feet one of the most puzzling clues was found—a stone marked with strange scratches. There are those who claim that the marks are some form of writing, but there are others who scoff at the idea and believe that the marks were made by the tools of the excavating team.

It is here that fantasy begins to run riot.

Both the Zeno brothers and Lord Sinclair had connections with the Knights Templar who had fought in the Holy Land. There are those who believe that their voyage had purposes other than just exploration, that Sinclair and the Zenos may have transported some of the Templars' treasure to Nova Scotia where it was buried on Oak Island for safekeeping. The favoured theory is that one of the items taken to Nova Scotia was no less than the Holy Grail itself and that it lies deep in the ground of Oak Island.

We now come forward some 600 years in time and to the arrival of 1300 Italians on the Orkney Islands. There is no fantasy here, just plain uncontested historical facts.

The Italian Chapel

The islands which go to make up the group known as the Orkneys off the northern coast of Scotland are roughly set out in the form of an inclined oblong. At the southern end of that oblong the islands form a sheltered lagoon with four major outlets to the open sea. For many years that lagoon, Scapa Flow, was one of the main anchorages of the Royal Navy and was strategically important as a base from which the Navy could control areas of the North Sea and the Atlantic ocean. It was at Scapa Flow that the entire German Navy surrendered to the British at the end of the First World War, and it was here in June 1919 that the same German Navy scuttled most of its ships to prevent them falling into Allied hands.

The surrender of the fleet at Scapa Flow had remained as a blot on the reputation of the German Navy and etched a scar on the psyche of the German nation. Adolf Hitler was acutely aware of this, and at the beginning of the Second World War he ordered the leader of the German fleet, Admiral Doenitz, to make a symbolic attack of some sort at Scapa Flow to erase the memory of the German surrender and scuttling of 20 years before. The man chosen by Doenitz to carry out the mission was a young submarine commander, Lieutenant Gunther Prien, who with his U-47 submarine had already notched up several sinkings of British merchantmen in the first few weeks of the war. Lieutenant Prien set out immediately, and shortly after 1.00 a.m. on the morning of 14 October 1939, Prien's U-47 threaded its way silently through the sunken blockships which guarded the four main entrances to Scapa Flow, then lay on the ocean bed to wait for daylight to pick out a suitable target. As dawn broke, the submarine rose quietly to the surface, where through his periscope Lieutenant Prien could observe several British warships at anchor. Half a mile away he noted a battleship, which he identified from his lists of British navy vessels as being the *Royal Oak*, a 31,200-ton battleship veteran of the Battle of Jutland more than 20 years before. Old though she was, he observed from his notes that she had been re-equipped and now was armed with eight 15-inch guns and protected by new armour plating. Lieutenant Prien manoeuvered his U-47 into position and fired three torpedoes at her. Aboard the *Royal Oak* most of the crew was asleep when three muffled explosions startled them awake. Moments later the entire ship exploded, sank like a stone and the lives of 833 seamen had been blotted out. Since she was anchored in the 'safe' waters of Scapa Flow, many doors, ventilators and hatches had been left open, and if these had been closed at the time of the attack, the *Royal Oak* would have taken longer to sink and possibly many lives would have been saved. The first British capital ship to be lost in the war, the *Royal Oak* lies on the sea bed on her port side in 25 metres of water, 1,000 metres from the shore. To this day the site of her sinking remains an official war grave and every year, on 14 October, a remembrance ceremony takes place and a White Ensign is placed on the hull by Royal Navy divers.

His mission accomplished, and as quietly and as surreptitiously as he had entered, Lieutenant Prien threaded his way out of Scapa Flow, avoiding the blockships and other defences, and by the morning of 15 October his U-47 had returned to the docks at Wilhemshaven, where Prien and his crew were met in triumph by Admiral Doenitz. Gunther Prien's achievement was a remarkable one, and probably one of the greatest feats ever carried out by a submarine in wartime. Given the relatively primitive underwater navigation equipment available on a wartime U-Boat, Prien's navigational skills in penetrating Scapa Flow were nothing short of miraculous. Historians now say that he must have been in possession of charts which marked out the defences of the lagoon, but even if that is so, and there is no mention of any such charts in his detailed logbook, the underwater navigational skills required for the action were remarkable. The crew of U-47 were awarded the Iron Cross on the spot for their exploit, and on the following day Hitler himself pinned the coveted Ritterkreuz—the Knight's Cross of the Iron Cross—on Prien's uniform. He called the Scapa Flow raid 'the proudest deed that a German U-Boat could possibly carry out.'

That exploit made Prien and his crew overnight sensations in Germany and established all U-Boat crews as heroes in German public opinion for the rest of the war. His feat in sinking the *Royal Oak* is made all the more remarkable by the fact that during the four and a half years of the Second World War only three battleships were ever sunk by submarine action: HMS *Royal Oak*, HMS *Barham* and the Japanese IJN *Kongo*. In the case of the latter two, the sinkings took place on the high seas and did not involve the navigating skills shown by Prien in breaching the defences of Scapa Flow. In his brief career before he himself was killed in 1941, Lieutenant Prien with his U-47 went on to sink 30 merchant vessels totalling 164,953 tons. He and the

U-47 were lost on the night of 7 March 1941, sunk by depth charges from the destroyer HMS *Wolverine* while the submarine was attacking a convoy of ships in the North Sea. Gunther Prien is also remembered for the sinking in June 1940 of the prison ship *Arandora Star* off the west coast of Ireland with the loss of 700 lives, of which more later.

The Admiralty in London were stunned by the news that the safety of the supposedly impregnable Scapa Flow had been breached, and commissioned a plan to block off the approaches to the lagoon anchorages. Churchill immediately decided to make the place impregnable beyond doubt, and to that end ordered the building of artificial barriers over the waters between the islands. These were to serve a dual purpose. It would be impossible for any submarine to penetrate the naval base, and at the same time, by building roads on top of the barriers, the many islands which go to make up the Scapa Flow anchorage would be linked together. The construction company Balfour Beatty were contracted to carry out the project of laying four massive concrete causeways across the seas through which Prien and his U-47 had entered the Scapa Flow base. These causeways were to become known as the Churchill Barriers. For such a vast undertaking a large workforce was required. Manpower was in short supply in wartime Britain, so every source of labour was considered. One great untapped source of manpower was the huge number of Italian soldiers who had been made prisoner in the North African campaign in 1941 and who were being housed in a string of POW camps stretching from North Africa to India. At the end of that year, 1,350 of these prisoners were brought to the Orkneys for the express purpose of building the Churchill Barriers.

One of the articles of the Geneva Convention states that prisoners of war must not be employed in military work of any kind, but in times of expediency all governments tend to ignore such niceties, and the Italian prisoners and their officers, who probably had no knowledge of the *Royal Oak* sinking, were told simply that the purpose of the causeways was to link the islands together by road. 800 of these POWs were housed in a camp on the island of Burray, and the remainder, 350 of them, in a camp on Lamb Holm Island. In this camp, known as Camp 60, the accommodation consisted of 13 Nissen huts set down on a barren piece of land and surrounded by barbed wire. The Italian prisoners were not long in tidying up their surroundings, planting flower beds and using left-over concrete from the causeway work in the building of paths to connect their huts and to cover the bare earth of the camp. One of the prisoners, Domenico Chiochetti, an artist from the little town of Moena in the Trento district of Northern Italy, who was skilled in painting and sculpture, conceived the idea of a statue to decorate the court-yard area of the camp. He obtained permission from the Camp Comman-dant, and created a remarkable statue of St George slaying the dragon. The statue, which stands to this day, was fashioned from concrete set around a base of barbed wire and wire netting, all waste products from the causeway construction work, which made the work all the more remarkable. The prisoners soon had other amenities for the camp under construction. Permis-sion was given for a recreation area, and a Nissen hut was converted for this purpose, complete with a billiard table fashioned out of concrete.

Balfour Beatty, who were still in charge of the overall work on the cause-ways, used the talents of some of the Italians in other ways, and employed the skills of two Ferrari mechanics in their motor transport workshop. In 1943 a new commandant, Major Buckland, was appointed to the camp, and since work on the causeways was now finished, he agreed to the request of the military padre, Father Giacobazzo, to have one of the Nissen huts con-verted into a chapel. On the understanding that only materials locally avail-able should be used in the project, the prisoners were given the use of two Nissen huts joined together, and construction began on what was to become a work of art which in future years would bring tourists to the Orkneys from every part of Europe and beyond.

Domenico Chiochetti took charge of the undertaking and he allowed his artistic imagination and creativity to run free. What eventually emerged was a remarkable work of art. The artist from the little town of Moena had nothing to work with except materials that were to all intents and purposes useless pieces of scrap, but he was able to bring together a team of his fellow prisoners with particular skills who were as enthusiastic about the project as he was, and who were willing to use whatever came to hand to convert the metal Nissens into a place of worship. Among them were two electricians, Primavera and Micheloni; a metal worker, Palumbo, who had worked as a founder in a Turin factory before the war; and Bruttapasta, who was skilled in the use of moulding cement and terrazzo. For months the group devoted all of their free time to the new project, and using any material that came to hand they started on the transformation of the two Nissen huts. There was a mountain of waste material to choose from. Tons of cement left over from the building of the causeways was available. Wire netting, metal rods used to strengthen the cement, and an assortment of jetsam from sunken ships lit-tered the beaches. Making use of these materials, the rippled metal interior of the Nissen huts was smoothed over with a cement and plaster covering; the altar, the railing, the holy water basin, all designed by Chiochetti, were modelled in cement reinforced by wire mesh by Buttapasta and his helpers. Images of St Francis and St Catherine were painted on the glass of the two windows, and on the plastered space above the altar, Chiochetti in the space of a few weeks painted a Madonna and Child, copied from a little holy picture which he always carried with him.

The Chapel was beginning to take form, and as the work progressed other prisoners came forward to help. The metal worker Palumbo put his skills to work. He gathered up some brass rods thrown onto a beach from a sunken ship, and fashioned two candelabra from them. Close by, and possibly from the same sunken ship, a large piece of mahogany wood was found, and this was put to use by a woodworker in the construction of a tabernacle. In the meantime, Chiochetti had decorated the plastered vault of the apse with the figures of the Apostles surrounded by angels. The contrast between the decorated section and the rest of the hut, which had remained untouched, gave Palumbo the idea of separating the two sections by means of a wrought iron grid, and again he created a work of art from the reinforcing rods of concrete blocks. No more unused rods were forthcoming, so surplus reinforced concrete blocks were smashed with hammers to free the sustaining rods, which were then fashioned into the intricate design they now present. His companion Primavera was able to find more brass rods thrown up by the tides, and four more candelabra were produced from the salvaged metal.

The first part of the hut to be decorated was the chancel, which can be considered to be the most beautiful part of the Chapel. The corrugated iron of the structure was covered by plasterboard, with an air space behind to guard against condensation, and an altar with altar rail and holy water font were moulded in concrete, again reinforced by wire netting. Behind the altar and sandwiched between two windows of painted glass, representing St Francis of Assisi and St Catherine of Siena respectively, Chiochetti painted his masterpiece and perhaps the defining part of the Chapel. This is a fresco done on a base of cement and plaster, with symbolic images of peace and friendship, and is after the style of the 'Madonna of the Olives' by the nineteenth-century Italian artist Nicolo Barabina.

After creating such decorative images in one part of the hut, Chiochetti and his craftsmen now realised how bare the rest of the Chapel was, so the rest of the hut was now covered in plasterboard, taking care to leave air spaces to isolate it from the metal behind. The plasterboard was then painted to resemble the interior of a church, with painted bricks at the top and a dado along the base to resemble carved stone. There was little else with which to decorate the Chapel, but the prisoners persevered in their search for materials, and using whatever scraps of usable junk they came across, the Chapel gradually took shape. The lanterns were made from bully beef tins hammered flat then beaten into the required shape, and the wire used to suspend them from the ceiling was cut from wire cables thrown up from sunken ships. In fact, the only items bought in for the Chapel and not made by the prisoners themselves are a pair of gold curtains, on either side of the altar, which were bought with money from the prisoners' own welfare fund. The interior was nearing completion, and so some thought was given to the outside of the structure, which was still merely an elongated Nissen hut. Chiochetti drew a plan, and the cement worker Buttapasta translated his sketch into an elegant facade with two slender columns forming a portico at the entrance, and a final thick covering of cement over the whole of the exterior of the huts finished the transformation. This done, the whole of the outside of the structure was painted over to resemble brickwork.

The end of 1943 brought about the downfall of Mussolini and the end of the war as far as Italy and the prisoners in the Orkneys were concerned, and the prisoners were preparing to be sent home. Chiochetti, after his years as a prisoner of war, was as eager as any of his colleagues to return to his home and family, but so taken up was he with his creation that he asked for permission to stay on in the Orkneys until his work was finished. When the Chapel was finally completed in the following year and he was ready to return home to Moena, Sutherland Graham, Lord Lieutenant of the islands, promised him that the chapel, which by now had been consecrated by the local bishop, would be properly maintained. To that end, a commission composed of local councillors to oversee the preservation of the Chapel was set up, and visitors who were by now flocking to the Chapel to see the marvel that had been created out of nothing were asked to give donations to help in the work of maintenance.

The fame of the remarkable Italian prisoner-of-war chapel in the Orkneys was spreading rapidly throughout the world, and in 1960 the BBC produced a programme which told the story of how a handful of Italian POWs had created a work of art out of a couple of Nissen huts and a pile of discarded junk. In the same year the BBC arranged for the return of Domenico Chiochetti to the island to supervise restoration work to his creation. His return to the place of his wartime imprisonment was warmly greeted by the inhabitants, and after several weeks of restoration work the Chapel was rededicated in the presence of over 200 of the local inhabitants. The bond that was established between the Orkneys and the town of Moena in the

Trento region of Italy by the building of the Chapel lasts to this day. The priest who celebrated the rededication of the shrine, Father Whitaker, finished his sermon with these words:

> 'Of all the man-made structures that were built on Lambholm during the war, only two remain, this Chapel and the statue of St George. All that was built for man's material needs has vanished, but these two, created to satisfy the spiritual needs of men, remain.'

Throughout the years many thousands of visitors have come to marvel at this extraordinary monument to the spirituality of man, built at the height of a savage war on a remote island in the North Atlantic, by a group of Italian prisoners in the middle of the POW camp which was their home from 1942 until early 1945. Chiochetti returned to the Orkneys again in 1964 with his wife, and gifted to the Chapel the 14 wooden Stations of the Cross which are on view today. Fifty years after the Italians were originally brought to Orkney, eight of the former prisoners returned in 1992, but Chiochetti was by now too ill and frail to travel with them. He died on 7 May 1999 in his home village of Moena, aged 89, in the knowledge that his masterpiece will live on as a tribute to his artistry. The Chapel stands also as a monument to the spirituality of his captors who, in the middle of a cruel war, gave permission for the work to be carried out, and to all those who worked on its construction and preservation.

During his last visit, before leaving for Moena after completing some repairs to his work, he wrote a letter to the people of the Orkneys in which he said:

> 'The Chapel is yours—for you to love and preserve. I take with me to Italy the remembrance of your kindness to me as a prisoner and the wonderful hospitality of this visit. I shall remember you always, and my children shall learn from me to love you. I thank you for having given me the joy of seeing again the little Chapel of Lamb Holm where I, in leaving, leave a part of my heart.'

❀ 4 ❀

The Beginnings

1876 was the first year in which records were started in order to catalogue the flow of immigration into the UK, and the information available to us shows that it was in the second part of the nineteenth century that the so-called chain migration phenomenon began. This was the name given to the process whereby the first immigrants to enter the country and settle in any given area, after having established themselves in work, sent for relations and friends to join them in their new country. Moreover, as the immigrant became established to the extent of opening his own small business or shop, he would seek workers from his own region or village. Persons from his own cultural background and language were easier dealt with than the locals, and since it was relatively easy to steal from the cash in circulation in these shops, workers from his own village or district could be trusted more than anyone from the sea of strangers around him. This was not because they were any more honest than anyone else, but because the immigrant worker, from the same village or hamlet as his employer, could never face up to the shame of being sent home for having stolen from his benefactor.

It was in this way that the formation of ethnic groupings of peoples of similar origins in towns and cities began. Towards the end of the nineteenth century, with the expansion in Europe of a railway and mass-transportation network, together with the development of the steamship which made sea travel faster and safer under bearable conditions, immigration speeded up considerably. (It has to be remembered that prior to the arrival of the steamship, long sea journeys in a sailing ship were a slow ordeal, which many a passenger did not survive.) According to the British census, the Italian presence in Great Britain quadrupled from 6,832 in 1881 to 24,383 in 1901, but no separate statistics are available for their number in Scotland. By comparison to the massive flow of immigration towards the Americas, both North and South, the number of Italians who came to settle in Britain was minute, and their distribution throughout the country followed no set pattern. The majority, of course, settled in the London area, where the cosmopolitan atmosphere and the existence of an already sizeable Italian presence acted as a magnet, and some made their way to Wales and into Lancashire.

Many Italian families travelled further on to Scotland, and in the industrial belt which stretches from Glasgow to Edinburgh, hundreds of Italian families made their homes and became a familiar part of the Scottish scene. A census taken in 1931, by which year every Alien in the country had to be registered and in possession of an Alien's registration book, shows that 4,100 Italians were registered in Scotland, and throughout the land there was hardly a village, town or city which did not boast of an Italian café or chip shop. However, Italian enclaves along the lines of a Soho in London or the Little Italy section of New York where Italians lived together as a group did not exist in either Glasgow or Edinburgh, where the bulk of Italian immigrants to Scotland had settled. In these cities the immigrant, having gone through a difficult learning process where a strange language and equally strange customs had to be learned, would set up a little business, usually a fish and chip shop or ice-cream café in an area where such a business might do well. They would set up home as close to their place of work as possible, usually in a tenement flat above the shop, and usually quite far removed from other Italian families.

Although many had travelled to Scotland overland from England, many of these immigrants also came by steamship, some to the North Sea port of Portobello and some to Glasgow. Many had been tricked by unscrupulous steamship agents into believing that they were on their way to the Americas, and had scraped up or borrowed the required fare for the journey, only to be disembarked at Portobello or Leith to find themselves ashore in the mistaken belief that they were in America. These people had no-one to turn to for assistance, but would always find shelter and help from the local parish priest, whose counterpart back home had as likely as not provided financial assistance for the journey. Until 1914, passports as we know them now did not exist, and since people could move freely without hindrance from one country to another, the unloading of such human cargo from these ships went unchecked by the authorities. However, as long as work is available and if he has no connections elsewhere, one country is as good as another for an immigrant, and many of these unfortunates with no family ties outside their homeland went no further and stayed on in Scotland.

The rapid growth of international transport systems by land and by sea made it necessary for governments to have some form of control over the increasing influx of migrants, so at the beginning of 1914, just before the outbreak of the First World War, the first modern passport was introduced, without which entry into the country would not be granted. Further to control and record the movement of foreigners, at the end of the First World War an Aliens act was passed by the UK Parliament which required all aliens over the age of 16 to register with the police, to carry an Alien's identity book and to report to them any change of address or circumstances, a requirement which remained in force until 1960 when the act was repealed.

From the Italian perspective of that era, the flow of emigrants from their native land was seen as the odyssey of a people in desperate search of a fresh life in unknown lands, and a retreat from a social system which offered them no hope of betterment. With hunger, poverty and social injustice at home as the spur, a massive flow of millions of Italians began to make their way to far-off lands which offered opportunity and the possibility of great wealth. Until the unification of Italy in the 1860s, no statistics were available to catalogue such an unprecedented movement of people, but between 1880 and 1890 it is recorded that some five million Italians left their homeland. In the first 20 years of the twentieth century a staggering total of ten million souls quit their native Italian regions to settle, for the main part, in the USA and the countries of South America. USA was the magnet, the country of choice, for there the pavements were said to be paved with gold. To this day, a stroke of good luck on the part of an Italian can be greeted with the exclamation: '*Ho trovato L'America!*' (I've found America!) In all, in the one hundred years between 1876 to 1976, more than 26 million Italians moved from the land of their birth to other countries in Europe and the Americas, a staggering number which represents more than one third of the present population of Italy.

The modern and affluent Italy of the European Union has begun to create a legend out of what probably has been, in the history of nations, one of the biggest recorded movements of people away from the land of their birth. As a percentage of population, the mass exodus from Ireland in the nineteenth and early twentieth centuries was greater, but in absolute terms much smaller. In the Italian cities of today the bookshops are full of books on the subject of Italian emigration, and on their shelves there are countless picture books with reproductions of old photographs, old faded reproductions which even after more than a century can still grip one's attention. Pictured here are gaunt and hardy men and women laden with all their worldly possessions, some with children, some with cloth bundles, some with old suitcases made of fibre and cardboard and tied with rope or string. There are photographs of row upon row of steamships filled with entire families packed tight in third-class decks or in steerage. We can also see their documents and travel

tickets, discoloured with the passing of time, together with faded photographs of entire families posing in front of wooden shacks in America, or
smoke-blackened tenements in Glasgow. Perhaps too there is the faded image of a street vendor standing self-consciously in front of an ice-cream cart,
suitably clad in bowler hat and white apron. These and thousands of similar
images were sent to the families who had been left behind, as if to show their
relations back home that the separation from the land of their birth and from
their relatives had brought some material results. These photos give no impression of happiness, and no-one in them smiles, as would be the case in
group photographs of today. However there is in them the dignity and strength
of character of persons who had left behind them misery and poverty, and
who were possessed of a determination to take advantage of the opportunities which lay open before them, and which did not exist in the land of their
birth. It is often said that it is only the strong, the brave and the ambitious
who leave their homeland in search of work and fortune in strange and
faraway lands.

Little is known of these early emigrants, who were for the most part
itinerant vendors and unskilled labourers, together with a few craftsmen.
Since many were illiterate, they left no personal written record of their
motivations and their hopes, but such people could be found all the way
from Russia, where they helped to build and to decorate the Kremlin, to the
western seaboards of the USA and Canada, where, under the supervision of
Scottish engineers, they laboured side by side with Chinese coolies and labourers from a dozen other lands to lay railway tracks across prairies, to drive
tunnels through the Rockies, to build the Brooklyn Bridge in New York
and to lay down the roads which were to unite a new continent. Many were
temporary immigrants who returned to their homeland as soon as they had
earned a little money, but some stayed on in these lands, and the registers of
birth of many a western Canadian and American town in the late nineteenth
century contain Italian names of children born there.

In Italy, however, there is now arising a new generation with views critical of those who emigrated in such vast numbers. The view taken of a nation's history often changes with time, and succeeding generations, conditioned by the economic and political climate in which they have grown up,
will often challenge and attempt to change the generally accepted view of
their nation's past. I was recently on a visit to Barga, the beautiful hilltop
town in an area of Tuscany, which 80 and more years ago was left desolate
and almost uninhabited by the exodus of families to the four corners of the
earth, but is now a prosperous and attractive tourist area. I was seated in a

bar, reminiscing about the years gone by with a group of others of my own age who also were on a visit to the land we had emigrated from so many years ago. The subject came around to a discussion of the fact that that particular area had seeded almost every country of the western world with its emigrants. At another table close by was a group of youths, who had been listening with interest to the old men's conversation. One of them interjected.

'Those people who emigrated deserted the land of Italy,' he said. 'They deserted their Motherland for a softer life in easier lands, when they could have remained at home and developed and changed the land of their birth. They could have made things better here if they had stayed. Had they done so, the whole of the history of Italy would have been changed, and we might never have had a Mussolini and a destructive war.'

These affluent youngsters, reared on a diet of fast Ferraris, Armani and Ferragamo glitz and Serie A football teams, cannot have the slightest idea of what their Italy was like one hundred, or even fifty, years ago. It is impossible for a modern Italian or European to imagine the way of life in Southern Italy and in a few regions of the North at a time when ship after ship was leaving for distant lands with its human cargo of suffering and hope.

In certain parts of Italy 80 or 100 years ago, in the industrial triangle formed by Milan, Turin and Genoa and in the lush plain of Lombardy, standards of living were comparable to those of any middle European country, but as one traveled further south the scene changed dramatically, and in parts of Tuscany the conditions which drove so many to seek another life in distant lands began to manifest themselves. Barga, where so many Scots-Italians have their origins, in those days was an impoverished town which reflected the deprivation of the surrounding countryside.

The hills above and around Barga were dotted with hundreds of tiny hamlets whose inhabitants lived at a bare subsistence level, and whose way of life had not changed in a century. Most of the land above Barga was owned by an absentee landlord, Pietro Bertacchi, who let out little parcels of his huge estates to tenant crofters and their families. The bigger the family, the bigger was the croft offered, for everyone in the family, no matter how young, would work the land and thus the land could be made to produce more for the owner. The rental paid to Bertacchi was not in cash, but consisted of one half of everything the land yielded: olives, cured ham and meats from pigs, cheese from sheep and goats, milk products from the cow that grazed on every hamlet, and grain and wool, if the croft was big enough to sustain more than just a few sheep. At 800 to 1000 metres above sea level vines could not be grown on these crofts, and a grape harvest, which could have given the families some extra income, was denied them. These share-croppers who worked the land were known as *mezzadri* from the word *mezzo*, which means half.

Bertacchi's agents would go round his estates with trains of mules (there were no roads, just goat paths which even a mule found difficulty in negotiating) to collect his share of the produce, and whatever remained was for the crofter family to live on. They existed on what they produced. Barter was a common form of trading. One hamlet with a surplus of cheese would trade with another which had a surplus of grain, one with a surplus of wool would trade with another with a surplus of leather. A family with the skills to make wooden *zoccoli* (clogs) would trade with another which could make iron implements, and so on. Cash money was seldom used between families. To obtain cash would have meant the selling of some produce in Barga or in the Lucca valley beneath, and the lack of roads made this a daunting proposition.

One hamlet in the area which was relatively prosperous was that of Bacchionero (Blackwoods), my birthplace and the birthplace of my mother before me. It consisted of a group of four or five farm buildings set round a tiny piazza graced at one end by a small church. Mass was said there every Sunday by a priest who came from the parish of Renaio in the valley below riding on a mule, but who returned home after the service on foot, with the mule laden with offerings from his parishioners, eggs, cheeses, hams and, a great delicacy, chestnut flour. One day each week the church would serve as a school organised by the priest for those who wanted to learn how to read and write, and such was the hunger for literacy among these crofters that the church was always packed for these lessons with persons of all ages, from the very young to the very old, some of whom had trekked many kilometers to attend. The relative affluence of my mother's family, the Caranis, who had worked the land for generations for the Bertacchi family, was based on the fact that the few houses that made up Bacchionero had been built in the middle of a huge forest of chestnut trees which produced tons of chestnuts every year. The trees shed their load of chestnuts at the onset of autumn, and these had to be gathered immediately or else they would lie to rot on the ground or be carried off by the wildlife of the region.

Every year at chestnut gathering time scores of families would climb up to Bacchionero, either from the Lucca valley beneath or from the other side of the Apuan Alps, journeys of many miles made on foot over rocky and dangerous paths. Men, women and young children, they would all set themselves to the gathering of the precious chestnuts until mountains of them had accumulated in the area in front of the church. The harvest could last for a week or so, with the peasants sleeping in barns or stables or wherever could afford shelter from the cold autumn nights. The chestnuts were taken to a neighbouring farmhouse known as Carletti, named after the family who had originally lived there. Built on the steep side of a hill and with no livestock except a few pigs and chickens, Carletti produced nothing. It had a mill wheel driven by the power of a fast-flowing stream over which the house had been built, and to this wheel all the corn and grain and chestnuts of the neighbouring crofts were brought to be ground into flour. When the chestnut flour had been poured into sacks, one half of these were put aside for Bertacchi, ready for collection by his agents. The Santi family, who lived there in the early part of the twentieth century and who operated the mill, received payment in the form of some sacks of flour in addition to some cured meats and cheese or whatever else might be offered by those who had made use of the their mill. In 1943 the Santi family, who were my mother's in-laws, became the proud possessor of the first electric lighting to be seen in those parts, generated by a dynamo stripped from a German jeep ambushed by a group of partisans. The dynamo was fitted to the mill wheel drive and produced enough current to light a few low wattage bulbs.

Their work done, the chestnut harvesters would return home. Payment for their work consisted of as much flour as they could load on their backs, and father and mother and children, all heavily laden with as much as each could carry, took to the rocky paths with their loads, some to descend into the valley below and some to climb back over the Apuan Alps into the valleys there, a backbreaking journey of two or three days. In 1931, at the age of twelve, I spent a whole year in Bacchionero. I lived in one of those farm buildings, and with my two older cousins I helped to tend the sheep and milk the goats and the two cows which the hamlet boasted of. I helped to thresh wheat with a primitive contraption consisting of two pieces of wood joined together with a leather strap and swung hard on the wheat stalks lying on the ground, so as to separate the grains. I helped to load the landlord Bertacchi's share on to his agent's mules, and I still have clear memories of the departing chestnut harvesters, laden like beasts of burden with sacks of chestnut flour, winding their way along the hillside paths.

One half of the remaining flour was collected by Bertacchi's agents and my mother's family kept the rest, this to provide them with luxuries such as olives and wine, bartered for the chestnut flour by crofters from the Lucca valley below. The chestnut trees provided another source of income for Bacchionero. In the winter months old trees would be felled and the trunks and branches cut into logs and charred over open fires. The charred logs were then tied into bundles and sent to the valley below by means of a primitive one-way funicular cable, there to be sold as firewood. This had been the way of life in the hills above Barga for centuries, and was the way of life of tens of thousands of peasant families in the hills of Tuscany, a life of work and drudgery which kept body and soul together but offered no hope or opportunity for a better life in the future. The ruling political classes and landowners of the early twentieth century wanted no change, their life was orderly and comfortable. But for those who wanted change, a door had opened: emigration.

In the Italy south of Rome conditions were universally bad. Naples and Bari had begun to show some little signs of economic awakening, but elsewhere in the South in general the way of life had changed little over the long decades, and a deadly immobility reigned until the arrival of Mussolini, who tried to instil life into the zone by laying down the infrastructure for the development of some industry. A small minority of arrogant well-to-do families, mostly landowners, lorded it over all others, most of whom lived a life of abject poverty with no hope of betterment. Most people in the South lived in rural communities whose urban centres, even though of several thousand inhabitants, were merely large villages with a few taverns and even fewer shops. In many townships clean water was a luxury and in the rainy season mud made the unpaved dirt roads well nigh impassable. Winter was short, but in the barren mountains covering most of the South it was extremely harsh.

Heating in the winter was unheard of, and in the summer there was no relief from the fierce heat. Many of the coastal plains were malarial, child mortality in these areas was probably as high as 25%, and it was not until the advent of Mussolini with his much-publicized draining of the Pontine marshes in the late 1920s that improvements began to be made. Damp one-room dwellings served both as living quarters for humans and as stables for livestock. From Matera to Ponza thousands of people lived in caves, and the handful of teachers and priests who struggled to bring even a basic literacy to these regions were paid a pittance by the ruling classes and their corrupt and venal governments. In 1950 the fledgling United Nations published a treatise 'World Literacy at Mid-Century', in which it found that 50% of the population south of Rome were illiterate. In comparison to the conditions prevailing in those parts of Italy, the crofters of Tuscany could consider themselves as living in the lap of luxury. There is no exaggeration in the writings of Ignazio Silone and Carlo Levi when they describe the life of the poor in these regions.

These are the words of Levi written in 1935 as he talks of Eboli, a town some 50 miles south of Naples where he was exiled for his left-wing political views and for having criticized the government of Mussolini. The amenities of that part of Italy were such that the government considered exile there a worse punishment than a prison cell.

'This land cut off from history, a land without comfort or solace, where the peasant lives out his motionless civilization on barren ground in remote poverty and in the presence of death. "We're not Christians," the people here say. "Christ stopped before he arrived here in Eboli." (In their way of speaking a "Christian" means "human being".)

Christ did stop at Eboli, where the road and the railway leave the coast of Salerno and turn into the desolate reaches of Lucania. Christ never came this far, nor did time, nor the individual soul, nor hope, nor the relation of cause to effect, nor reason nor history. Christ never came, just as the Romans never came, content to garrison the highways without penetrating the mountains and forests, nor the Greeks, who flourished beside the Gulf of Taranto. None of the pioneers of Western civilization brought here his sense of the passage of time and no one has come to this land except as an enemy, a conqueror, or a visitor devoid of understanding. The seasons pass today over the toil of the peasants, just as they did three thousand years before Christ; no message, human or divine, has reached this stubborn poverty. A different language is spoken here and that language to me is incomprehensible. Here the furthest travelled has not gone beyond the limits of his own world; here they have trodden the paths of their own souls, of good and evil, of morality and redemption. Christ came down from heaven to redeem humanity for all eternity. But to this shadowy land, that knows neither sin nor redemption from sin, where evil is not moral but is only the pain residing forever in earthly things, Christ did not come. Christ stopped at Eboli.'

The economy of the South, such as it was, was based almost entirely on agriculture, with manufacturing industry almost non-existent. Three out of every five persons were classified as agricultural workers, and the supply of labour was twice as much as the demand, hence chronic unemployment and widespread under-employment reigned. Those looking for work could expect no more than one hundred days' employment in the year, and some worked not at all. In the area of 22 million acres encompassing what had been the kingdom of the two Sicilies before unification and of which Levi speaks, 21 million of these acres were owned by the aristocracy and the upper middle classes. The remaining one million acres was shared by one and a half million tenant peasants, giving each an average of just over half an acre to live on and to cultivate, this on land where yields were low and where barely enough could be harvested to keep a family alive. Moreover, Italy south of Naples lived in the strangling grip of an octopus which choked off all possibility of change, the Camorra of Naples, the N'drangeda of Calabria, and most powerful and all-embracing of all, the Mafia of Sicily.

Such conditions were not always accepted with resignation. There were often bloody uprisings, strikes and protest gatherings by the peasant classes which were always ruthlessly put down. As recently as May Day of 1947 a protest gathering of several thousand land workers and crofters in Sicily at a place named Porta della Ginestra was fired upon by a Mafia group hired by the local landowner. Twelve in the crowd were killed, including women and children, and many more wounded. Those Italians of the generations of today who are critical of the emigrants of one hundred years ago and after, should be made to understand the bleak history of their own now–affluent land.

❀ 5 ❀

Immigration

Where is the Tally's that I knew so well?
That corner shoppie where they used to sell
Hot peas, a maccallum, ice-cream in a poke,
You knew they were Tallies the minute they spoke.
Adam McNaughtan

The first Italians to come in any sizeable number to Scotland in the 1820s and 30s were a trickle who came north from the little Italian enclave of Clerkenwell in London, where hundreds of Italians had already settled. Many of these were craftsmen, mosaic workers and stonemasons skilled in the art of stone reproductions of heroic statues of antiquity, such as can still be seen supporting the portals of many a London building of the nineteenth century. Of the ones who drifted away from the London enclave, some were organ-grinders and street entertainers, and some were sellers of little plaster statuettes, '*figurini*', as they were known, reproductions of the Madonna and of the saints, of the Leaning Tower of Pisa, of Michelangelo's David and others which they hawked from door to door. They were street vendors who had been recruited in Italy by a local Padrone, or Boss, and who were pledged to work for their employers for a specified period of time.

These sellers of *figurini* came in the main from the Lucca area, where the art of copying the numberless works of art to be found in the Lucca–Pisa–Florence zone of Tuscany had been developed by local craftsmen. These little statuettes were produced by the thousands and sold from door to door in the countries north of the Alps by groups of youths, sometimes only in their early teens, under the supervision of a 'Padrone', or 'Capo' who himself was answerable to another Padrone or Capo back in the homeland. With them came the *arrotini*, or knife grinders, who sometimes accompanied the statuette sellers on their rounds and who did a brisk trade by sharpening knives in the hundreds of grocer and butcher shops which were beginning to appear in the streets of the towns and cities of Northern Europe, and who needed their tools of trade attended to. Occasionally in their company would be also unskilled labourers with nothing but their muscle and brawn to offer, and who always managed to find some form of work on their travels.

Amongst them too were a few budding entrepreneurs who were quick to see the opportunities that existed in the new lands opening up before them. These enterprising ones in their turn became Padroni who realised how their fellow nationals could be used to create little business empires to their mutual benefit, and how they themselves could progress from being itinerant pedlars and vendors to full-fledged shopkeepers.

One such Padrone was Carlo Gatti, from an Italian speaking canton of Switzerland, who had acquired his sales expertise by peddling statuettes from door to door in France. There, on the Cote d'Azur, he had watched ice-cream being made and sold in the streets and in bars, and had brought his knowledge to London where he had emigrated to in the late 1840s. There he set up business selling refreshments and ice-cream from a cart in the summer and roast chestnuts from the same cart in the winter. The making of ice-cream depends on a supply of ice to freeze the ice-cream mixture, and this was obtained in the winter by cutting it from frozen lakes and ponds and packing it deep in straw in some kind of insulated room, which usually consisted of a deep cellar or suchlike. With the provision of drainage to carry off water, ice could be stored in this manner for months, some say years, and Gatti obtained his ice in the winter from the Regent Canal and stored it in this way. He was so successful in selling ice-cream from his gaudily decorated barrow that he thought up the idea of obtaining more carts, and of hiring men and sending them out to sell his product in the streets of London. To produce ice-cream in this kind of quantity he needed a far bigger supply of ice than he could ever cut from local sources, so he arranged for the bulk import of ice from Norway. Ice had been exported from Norway to London since the beginning of the 1800s, when it was sold to restaurants, butchers and fishmongers to keep their foods chilled and reasonably fresh.

To store and preserve such large quantities of ice, large specially insulated structures known as ice wells, capable of storing many hundreds of tons of it, were built in New Wharf Street. Gatti reserved a space in a New Wharf Street ice-well and stocked 400 tons of ice there on hand to be used for the manufacture of his ice-cream. These ice-wells remained in use until 1902, by which time mechanical production of ice had become possible, and since it could now be produced on demand, such ice storehouses were no longer needed. Gatti then began to import labour from Italy, and various Padroni there provided him with a flow of willing and unsophisticated labour. These immigrants were recruited in large part from the Ciociara region south of Rome, and were mainly simple country folk whom he lodged in conditions not much better than those they were accustomed to back home. After a brief training they were sent out to sell ice-cream in the streets, and during the winter when it was too cold for the sale of ices they worked as hurdy-gurdy men or converted their ice-cream barrows to serve as hot chestnut stalls, and for all this they were paid a pittance. In summer every morning they poured the ice-cream liquid mix they had prepared the previous night into a deep round metal cylinder surrounded by chipped ice brought up from the Wharf Street storage. The ice packed around the cylinder was mixed with salt, thus dropping the temperature, then the container was rotated round and round by hand until the mixture had solidified into ice-cream. They then went the rounds of the streets of the city, ringing a bell or blowing a whistle and shouting out, 'Gelati, ecco un poco!'('Ice-cream, here's a little!') It is thought to be because of this cry that ice-cream vendors were called 'hokey pokey men'.

Most books are full of myths and conjecture as far as the history of ice-cream is concerned. According to many popular accounts, the Venetian explorer Marco Polo saw frozen milk mixtures of various flavours being made during his wanderings in China at the beginning of the fourteenth century, and on his return to Venice introduced them to Italy. Before Marco Polo's time there are references in Roman writings to the emperor Nero, who ordered ice to be brought from the mountains to cool sweetmeats decorated with fruit toppings, and in later centuries recipes for ices, sherbets, and milk ices evolved and were served in the fashionable Italian and French royal courts. Whatever the origin and history of ice-cream might be, the ice-cream on offer by the Italian street vendors in London was sold in small drinking glasses called 'penny licks', because the customer had to lick the ice-cream from the glass container, which was used over and over again without washing, and it cost a penny to do so. No one bothered much about hygiene or the lack of it in those days, but the problem for the vendors was that some people would accidentally break the glasses, or quite simply run off with them. Italian ice-cream street sellers were also active at that time in New York, where the penny lick was also on offer, and there a street vendor named Italo Marcioni solved the problem of the breaking and pilfering of his penny lick glasses.

His first solution was to make cone-like containers out of paper and serve the ice-cream in them. This allowed him to do away with glass containers, but his customers were at times not happy with the soggy mixture of melting ice-cream and paper they had to hold in their fingers and so, with a flash of genius, he thought of a new possibility. He came up with the idea of making an edible container for his merchandise and in 1896 he began producing edible wafer cups with sloping sides shaped like a drinking glass, and thus the ice-cream cone was born. The idea spread rapidly to the UK and Europe, and since he had taken out a patent on his invention he became a wealthy man. The glass 'licks' remained in use in London until they were made illegal just before the First World War, for reasons of public health.

The trickle of immigrants into the UK became a sizeable stream by the 1880s. Recruited by agents working for Padroni in London, Italians were brought to Britain as cheap labour and some filtered north to Glasgow, where in 1890 a Padrone by name of Carlo Giuliani, who as a boy had worked as a street vendor for Gatti, had established three very successful cafés, two of which were located in Argyle Street near Glasgow Cross, and the third by the side of Glasgow Green. From these cafés he ran scores of ice-cream carts which he put in charge of these newly arrived immigrants, who again were mainly from southern Italian towns in the Frosinone province with names like Picinisco, Filignano, Atina and Cassino. They were given a barrow stocked by Giuliani with ice-cream and sweets and became 'hokey pokey' men trudging the streets of the city, or stationed at the entrance of public parks to sell their wares. Handling these ice-cream barrows was back-breaking work, and to push one up even a slight incline required a lot of muscle. There are many areas in Glasgow which are quite hilly; the district around Queen's Park, a popular district for ice-cream barrows, was particularly steep, and the vendors there could not manage to push the carts up the inclines without help and had to rely on the help of local youngsters, who would be given a 'pokey hat' for an assist to the top of the slope.

Giuliani's Glasgow Green Café did a roaring trade, and was particularly successful. That was the age of open-air public oratory, when anybody with a political or a religious message to convey to his fellow citizens could stand on a soap-box or suchlike in a public place and harangue away to his heart's content. Glasgow Green was the traditional venue for the speakers who orated there every Sunday. Thousands gathered outside to listen to them and Giuliani's café had no less than five counter assistants helping to attend to the crowds of customers queuing up to be served. A favourite drink of the day was a concoction of carbonated water flavoured with fermented ginger known as ginger beer, which was prepared in the cellar of the café and then poured into stone bottles and sealed with a wired cork. These bottles were bought literally in their thousands by the thirsty customers at tuppence a time, with a penny return on the bottle, and it was rumoured that Giuliani's ginger beer had in it a small percentage of alcohol to make it that much more attractive. Giuliani is also credited with the invention of the so-called iced drink, a great favourite among café goers. This consisted of a ball of ice-cream put into a tall glass, stirred up with lemonade or ginger beer or some such soft drink and then sucked up through a straw. Legend also has it that he invented the 'maccallum', the name given to a ball of ice-cream topped with raspberry sauce, although why that particular concoction should go by such a name is unknown. Until very recently, and perhaps even now, customers would go into an ice-cream shop and ask for a 'maccallum'. In the winter months there was little or no sale of ice-cream, so hot drinks of the Bovril type, or hot lemonades or hot chocolate were offered up for sale. Hot peas, served in deep plates, then seasoned with pepper and vinegar, were a favourite dish consumed in great quantities by his customers. In the absence as yet of 'artificial' ice, in winter many of Giuliani's workers were given the task of cutting ice from the upper reaches of the Clyde and storing it in the Glasgow equivalent of the Wharf Street ice-wells, an ice store in the Broomielaw close by the Fish Market, where it would be retrieved in summer for the making of his ice-cream.

Italians have long had the reputation of being highly individualistic and not taking kindly to having others benefit from the fruits of their labour, and so eventually, as more and more of the immigrants became acquainted with the language and customs of their new homeland, many broke away from their Padroni and began to open up their own little shops around the city, and so the ice-cream barrows slowly began to vanish from the city streets, eventually to be seen only at the entrance to public parks or at football matches on Saturdays. As likely as not, the disappearance of a barrow would be followed immediately by the opening of an ice-cream shop just a few yards away, owned by the erstwhile street vendor. An example of this can be seen at two of the gates of Queen's Park in Glasgow. At the Victoria Road entrance, in the early 1920s, the barrow which always stood there in summer was replaced by the Queen's Café, opened by the Iacconelli family, a café which is still operative to this day. At the Pollokshaws Road entrance around the same time, the ice-cream barrow there was replaced by the state-of-the-art Bluebird café, a sumptuously equipped ice-cream parlour whose ice-cream became famous throughout Glasgow, and which only recently was converted to an Indian restaurant.

It cost very little to set up a shop then, given that in the poorer districts only the basic amenities for customers needed to be provided and sanitary considerations were not of paramount importance. All that was required to set up that type of business was a wooden counter over which to serve the public and some kind of workshop at the back of the premises, which in the case of ice-cream shops would serve as a preparation room for the ice-cream mixture and in the case of the fish and chip shop as a place to peel potatoes and to gut and fillet fish. Town planning as far as the opening of shops of this nature was concerned did not exist. Once a site had been identified as having a potential for profit, such as being near a public park or playing field or Clyde ferry or a busy tram or bus stop or in a heavily populated district, the latter being almost everywhere in Glagow, the factor of the property would be approached and a lease negotiated. In the space of a few weeks a new ice-cream shop with a well-stocked window display, fitted out and decorated with due regard to the affluence of the area, would appear. Almost always a fish and chip shop would appear in close proximity, for a good site for the one was an equally good site for the other.

Giuliani began to open up little ice-cream shops throughout the city, and ran them by sending back to Italy and recruiting more immigrants from the poorer villages, again mainly in the Ciociara region. His agents there would go the rounds of the countryside, enticing suitable labour with glowing tales of the comfort and luxuries awaiting them in Glasgow, the wide streets, the theatres, the big shops, and of course, most important of all, the money that could be made by willing workers. On arrival, these *contadini*, or farm work-ers, since that was usually their background, were trained in the basics of the trade and taken on by him as full-fledged partners on an equal basis in the running of these new concerns. As far as the language went, they were left to their own resources to manage as best they could, and the fractured English or the Glasgow version of it that they learned to speak caused a great deal of merriment and derision amongst the locals they came into contact with. Giuliani would supply the newcomers with a fully fitted shop with all the necessary furniture and equipment, plus the usual stocks of cigarettes, choco-lates, soft drinks, milk and sugar and other raw materials needed for the manufacture of ice-cream. The working partner would provide the labour and see to the efficient running of the business, the profits being shared equally between them. After a time, the café would be offered for sale to the tenant and the number of ice-cream shops in the city of Glasgow began to increase, until there was hardly a district which did not have its own little corner café.

The work entailed long hours—a working day of 14 and 15 hours was normal—and the shops provided a living for the persons who worked them, but only just. What the immigrants had to learn by bitter experience was that the work in such shops was long and hard and that they had practically no time off to enjoy their new surroundings, since to make any kind of profit the shops had to be opened up early in the morning and closed at night as late as the law allowed, seven days a week. Nevertheless, life was always better than it had been back home, and since there were opportunities for personal betterment undreamt of in their previous existence, there was no shortage of willing volunteers for Giuliani's enterprises. Just how rapid the spread of these shops in Glasgow was is shown by police statistics which tell that in 1903 there were 89 ice-cream shops in the city, a year later there were 184 and by 1905 there were estimated to be 336 ice-cream shops in the Glasgow area. The Italian immigrant population had been growing just as quickly and reached a high point of 4,500-5,000 around this time, a figure which gradually diminished as more and more of the immigrants, having acquired a little money, returned home. A handful of those who decided to remain in their adopted land took out British citizenship and thus were removed from the Aliens list. The number of these alien Italian nationals in Glasgow then remained more or less stable at 4,000 or so until the outbreak of the Second World War.

Why it should be that the ice-cream and the fish and chip trades, as far as Scotland is concerned, were taken up almost in their entirety by Italians is a mystery. There are no Scottish-type ice-cream shops anywhere in Italy, neither are there any fish and chip shops as we know them here, and yet in Scotland in the early part of the twentieth century these trades were 99% in the hands of Italians and started by them. The explanation may lie in the fact that the native Scots were simply not prepared to work the long and anti-social hours necessary to carry on these trades. Eating deep-fried fish had become popular in London and the south-east by the middle of the nineteenth century. Charles Dickens mentions a 'fried fish warehouse' in *Oliver Twist*, and these establishments were usually run by Greeks who introduced the sale of baked potatoes to serve alongside the fried fish. Unlike the trend in Scotland, this trade was taken up and expanded by native Londoners, and there is no record of Italian-owned fish and chip shops in the London of that time. A publication of the day has this to say about the fish friers:

> 'The fried fish sellers live in some out-of-the-way alley, and not infrequently in garrets, for even among the poorest class there are great objections to their being fellow-lodgers on account of the odour of the frying. A gin-drinking neighbourhood suits

these fried fish shops best, for people don't bother much about smells there.'

It was not until the turn of the century that the trade began to develop as we know it now. The London County Council's records for 1906 show that there were 'a few fried fish shops' in the year of the Great Exhibition. At that time, it is recorded, the fish was commonly sold in conjunction with baked potatoes, but the practice of selling the fish with fried chipped potatoes had now been introduced from France. Hence the modern term 'French Fries'. A journalist of that time writing in the *Times* laments the passing of the baked potato thus:

> 'Butter and salt were available for the customer, and I, for one, greatly lament the passing of this warming and nutritious com-modity. It is hard to counterfeit the honest baked potato, but who knows what goes into the French fried substitute.'

What Giuliani did for the ice-cream shop in Glasgow another entrepre-neur Padrone called Primo Marchi did for the fish and chip shop. Primo Marchi, who, like Giuliani, came from the Barga area in Tuscany, arrived in Glasgow towards the end of the nineteenth century and set up a fried fish and chip shop along the lines of the ones he had seen during his brief stay in London. This stood on a site at the corner of Renfrew Street and Renfield Street, on a block later to be taken up by the Green's Playhouse cinema and later still by the modern UGC multicinema which stands there now. Primo Marchi's fish and chip shop, a large barn-like structure which could seat about 150 customers and with a separate carry-out department, set a trend, and like Giuliani's cafés, did a roaring business. Soon there were as many fish and chip shops to be seen in Glasgow as there were cafés, if not more. Many of these fish and chip shops had been opened up by Primo Marchi, who used the same methods as did his precursor Giuliani, setting them up, staffing them and then after a period selling them off or hiring them to his workers. The main difference was that whilst the great majority of the Giuliani hu-man imports came from the southern regions of Italy, almost all of Primo Marchi's labourers came from his home district, the Lucca-Barga zone of Tuscany, and for many years almost all fish and chip shops in Scotland were owned by northern Italians descended from the Marchi line, and the ice-cream cafés were all owned by persons from south of Rome deriving from the Giuliani strand.

Of the two trades, the fish and chip shop was by far the harder and the dirtier, entailing as it did the handling of hundredweight sacks of potatoes and boxes of fish made heavy by the packed ice inside, although the hand cranking of the metal freezers in the early ice-cream shops also required a great deal of brawn and stamina. Before the advent of electrically-driven potato-washing machines, potatoes had to be washed by hand, by rotating them in a metal cylinder equipped with water jets, and there was not much diffference in the effort required for either of these two primitive and back-breaking procedures. The fish and chip trade was by far the dirtier and smellier of the two. With the coming of electrically assisted machines the café owner did not need to soil his hands in the course of his day's work, but the fish frier never ceased to have his hands covered in grease, fish scales and batter and in coal dust too, from the handling of the coal which fired his cooking ranges. Not to mention the all-pervasive and distinctive smell created by the frying of the fish and of the chipped potatoes in hot beef dripping. This smell, which before the coming of modern extraction and filtering systems could lie like a blanket over the shop's immediate area, was difficult to remove from a person's clothing and body. Little wonder that the Glasgow City fathers were driven to classifying fish frying as being a 'noxious' trade, along with that of blood-boiler, bone-boiler, fell-monger(dealer in slaughtered hides), soap-boiler, tallow-melter and tripe-boiler. Special licenses, the pre-cursors of planning permission procedures, had to be granted for the open-ing of such premises. A Dr Ballard, a London public health inspector report-ing on the proliferation of fried fish shops in 1890, had this to say:

> 'This trade is a source of considerable nuisance in the neighborhoods in which it operates, the offensive smell of the oil boiling and the fish frying spreads often through the whole length of the street where the shop is situated. Pedestrians are annoyed by it, and so also are the persons who chance to reside in the neighbourhood. There is, I believe, scarcely a health of-ficer in London who has not at some time been called upon to advise as to an appropriate remedy for this nuisance.'

In 1940, the wartime government, anxious to keep open as many sources of food as possible for the public, lifted the 'noxious trade' classification, and actively encouraged the use of mobile fish and chip shops on wheels to serve country districts and housing estates, noxious smell and all.

As far as the prospective shop-owner was concerned, fish and chip shops had one great advantage over the ice-cream trade. They were by far cheaper to set up and required very little capital expenditure. With the outlay of just a little cash, a wooden counter could be erected in front of a large brick range on the top of which a circular space for a coal fire was left. A black iron pan some two feet and more deep could be moved back and forth over the hot coal, and into this pan you put half a hundredweight or so of dripping to fry the fish and chips and you were in business. You had to be strong and fearless to handle these deep frying pans. Filled to capacity with dripping and a large basket of chips or twenty or so fish, their weight was considerable, and they had to be moved back and forth over the hot coals to maintain them at the required temperature. The movement had to be smooth, for it required only a splash of hot fat over the edge for the whole contraption to erupt in flames. The fumes from the frying process were left to be dissipated into the atmosphere, to settle were they might. Dangerous though it was to operate those primitive fish-frying ranges, there is no record of any of them ever having caused a dangerous fire.

Moreover, unlike the cafés, which had to carry a fairly large stock of cigarettes and sweets, no such costly stock was required for the fish and chip shops. All that was needed to operate was a daily supply of a few stones of fish, a hundredweight or so of beef dripping, some flour to make a paste for the frying of the fish, and a few hundredweight sacks of potatoes, all of which could be bought on a daily basis with the proceeds of the previous day's business. Another advantage the chip shops had over the cafés was the shorter opening hours of the former. The café opening hours stretched from the early morning until midnight in some cases, with Sunday opening for them all, whilst the chip shop owner, once having prepared his potatoes and fish in the morning, could take the afternoon off until about 4 o'clock, when the doors would open in expectation of the teatime rush.

Most of these fish and chip shops closed on a Sunday, but the remaining six days of the week demanded unremitting hard work. The day started at 6 o'clock in the morning with a visit to the Fishmarket in the Briggate, as early as possible so as to pick and buy the best of the fish on offer. The boxes chosen would be marked with the buyer's particular sign, usually his shop street number, and then, once having seen them loaded onto the carrier's horse-drawn cart, after which they became the carter's responsibility, a vist to Cooper's coffee room in Howard Street for a coffee and a chat with one's fellow nationals was mandatory. The way from the fish market to Cooper's could have been found blindfolded, all one had to do was to follow the entic-ing odour of coffee coming from the coffee-grinding and roasting machine in Cooper's shop window. On the way there along Clyde Street a stop was often made at Fazzi's famous delicatessen at the suspension bridge for the purchase of some Italian food delicacy, or for some particular design of chip frying basket, various types of which hung suspended behind the counter. Then a cup of coffee or so later, enjoyed in front of a welcoming coal fire always alight in the coffee room, it was back to the shop to start the real work of the day. A few hundredweight of potatoes would be washed, peeled and cut into chips, either by hand with a knife or by means of a heavy guillotine-type potato cutter which required considerable strength and stamina to operate. Then the preparation of the fish, which by now the carter would have delivered to the shop premises, would begin. The fish used in most shops was usually haddock. Some of the shops in the poorer districts served whiting, a much cheaper fish which could lower the price of a fish supper from the sixpence charged in the better shops to fourpence.

The fish, once freed from their bed of chipped ice in the boxes, would be headed, gutted and filletted, often by hand with no recourse to a knife. Winter or summer, this required a pail of hot water to revive one's hands and fingers, numb with cold from the ice-cold fish. There were many fish friers who claimed that a fish with its bone extracted by the fingers, which left it with a rough texture rather than with the smooth flesh left by a filletting knife, made for a better fish supper. The claim was that the roughness left in the fish by tearing away the bone by hand trapped the tasty batter in which the fish was fried, and gave it a better flavour. This work could go on till midday or after. Once the work of preparation was finished, a hearty meal would follow, almost always some traditional Italian dish prepared by the woman of the house. After this a couple of hours of siesta was taken, then it was down to the shop to start the fires and prepare for the night's business. The busiest day of the week for the fish frier was a Friday. One third of the population of Glasgow was Catholic, mainly from the Irish flow of immigration in earlier years, and since Friday was a day of abstinence in the Catholic calendar, then on that day meat should not be eaten. The result was a long queue at the local fish and chip shop on Fridays. We can only speculate as to what the pious had to eat on days of abstinence before the coming of the fish and chip shop.

In addition to the long hours and hard and unpleasant work entailed and the objections from various groups of Glasgow citizens, there were other problems involved in running a fish and chip shop, or an ice-cream shop too, for that matter. Many, if not most, of these shops were situated in some of the poorer and tougher quarters of the city, and the immigrant behind the counter had to put up with a great deal of verbal and sometimes physical abuse from his customers. There was no race relations act to invoke if insulted or sworn at or assaulted by one's customers. These immigrant shopkeepers were called 'Tallies', a word which in itself was perhaps not abusive in a city whose working classes, and many who should have known better, referred to Catholics as 'Dans', Protestants as 'Billys' and Jews as 'Old tin cans', but very often it would be preceded by a stream of invective and adjectives of the four-letter type, which the shopkeeper had to learn to put up with in order to keep the peace. If anything, the fish and chip shops tended to be more difficult to run in that respect than the cafés. At pub closing-time the drunks, driven by their alcohol-induced hunger, would spill out onto the pavements and go in search of the nearest fish shop for a bag of chips or a fish supper to satisfy their appetite. Very often verbal abuse would be hurled at the hapless owner. Sometimes, though, the patient shopkeeper's acceptance of such abuse would reach breaking point, and the results were sometimes drastic. The immigrant, however, could always rely on the local police for assistance. The following quote is a from the reminiscing of an old policeman who patrolled a fairly tough beat in Parliamentary Road in the early thirties, as reported in *The Big Men*, my book about the Glasgow police who worked out of the Northern police division in the first part of the twentieth century:

'There was a Tally fella called Gino who ran the San Remo chip shop in the Parly Road, a real busy place, but a real tough shop it was. Gino was tough and strong, hard as nails he was, worked out with weights in McMillan's gym in Sauchiehall Street every day and sparred there with the likes of Elky Clark and Benny Lynch and Sandy McKenzie and was as strong as a bull and he never ran away from a fight. The local hard men knew what he could do and left him strictly alone. One night three stranger neds from the Garngad come in and start off, "Gie us three fish suppers, ya fuckin' Tally bastard." When they start off like that you know they're out for trouble and are no gonny pay for anything they get and are gonny give you a hard time and maybe finish off at the demand, so what does Gino do? He looks at them hard for a minute and disnay say a word back. He picks up a wee saucepan, dips it into the hot fat and throws the hot dripping in their faces, and when they're running about daft like burnt chickens yelling and screaming blue murder he goes out and blows hard on the whistle. Big Tam, my neighbour on the beat and myself are standing in West Nile Street and we hear the whistle go so we go along to see what was wrong and we run the three of them in for a breach of the peace. We had to take them to the hospital first to get fixed up though. Their faces were in a real helluva mess, all blistered up with the skin hanging off and they were greeting like weans. They got fined two quid each the next morning for a breach of the peace. They never went back, that taught them.

Gino was maybe a wee bit too rough at times at that, and he nearly killed a fella once. This one, a big bugger more than six feet tall, comes in and starts effing and ceeing at one of the counter girls for something or other and after a while Gino goes over and tells him to keep quiet. The bloke doesn't take a blind bit of notice and keeps on swearing at the lassie, worse than ever, so George tells him again to keep quiet. So this time he starts swearing at Gino instead and starts calling him a Tally cee and a this and that. Gino again disnay say a word but reaches up and grabs him by the collar with one hand and twists as hard as he could. The guy turns blue in the face and collapses frothing at the mouth and lies there stiff as a board. Gino gets a real big fright, he thought the guy was dead and he blows his whistle and when we get there we thought the guy was dead too, but just in case we call an ambulance and take the guy to the Royal and it turns out he's still alive, and he's let out the next day OK. The doctor said he was lucky, one more twist on the collar and he would have snuffed it. So we tell Gino that maybe he ought to take it a wee bit easier with the neds.'

The same policeman continues:

'There was a wee Tally called Andretti, a wee stout fella who had a wee carry out in St Georges Road, It was a busy wee shop, but it was rough and the neds used to come in at the demand. St George's Road wasn't the worst place in the world, but it was near the Garscube Road and the neds from there gave the Tallys a hard time of it. One day Andretti tells us that he's getting pestered with two neds at the demand who're giving him a lot of abuse and who are taking stuff away without paying. I partnered big John Scott at the time and he listened and said to the wee Tally:

"Don't give the bastards anything. Get hold of a club, and when they come in you show them the club and if they don't want to pay for anything or if they want some money at the demand you tell them to eff off or you'll bust their bloody head in. Buy yourself one of our whistles and if you get any trouble give us a toot and we'll sort them out."

So Andretti went to Crockett's in the Cowcaddens to buy a whistle, Acme Thunderers, they were called, and he got a club as well and he kept it hidden down at the side of the counter. One night we're standing at the Cross and we hear a whistle blowing like mad and it was coming from Andretti's shop. We go in and the place was a bloody mess, broken glass everywhere and there was a funny smell of burning. So we asked what had happened and Andretti said in his Tally accent:

"Well, they came in and asked for two fish suppers and when I asked them for the money they told me to fuck off and they wouldn't pay, so I brought the club out like you told me, and the two of them grabbed it with both hands; I think they were going to use it on me. The only thing was, it wasn't a club. It was a bloody iron bar, and I had kept an end of it in the fire, and the top of it was nearly red hot and the two of them left their bloody skin on it, it stuck to their hands and they started screaming blue murder and ran away."

So we went out and asked around and somebody told us they had gone home to get their hands fixed. We went up to the neds' house to arrest the two of them for a breach of the peace, and there they were with their hands stuck out in front of them covered in bandages, no able to do anything, being looked after by their wives and they're calling wee Andretti for everything. We got them hauled up in front of the magistrate and they were fined two pounds each for a breach of the peace. The wives had to take the money out of their pockets, they couldnay use their hands for weeks.'

Similar scenes were enacted night after night in cafés and chip shops, and the immigrant had to accept them as part of their way of life or else seek a different line of work to make a living.

Oddly enough, despite their comparative cleanliness and absence of smells and despite the fact that they were pleasant places for people to meet, in certain areas ice-cream cafés were subjected to a great deal of criticism by many Glaswegians, and attempts were made to have them closed and banned from the city. Glasgow in the nineteenth and early part of the twentieth century was a city which was run along strict Presbyterian moral lines. Everything shut down on a Sunday, for the Sabbath was a day meant for prayer and rest from labour and not for material activities, so when these foreign sellers of ice-cream, an unneccessary luxury it was maintained, desecrated the Sabbath by opening their doors on that day, howls of protest were raised and the cafés were decribed as being dens of iniquity which corrupted the morals of the young. The *Glasgow Herald* of 7 June 1906 carried an article by the British Women's Temperance Association with the title 'An Objectionable Trade', which argued that one of the most objectionable and pernicious aspects of Sunday trading in Scotland was that of the ice-cream shop, which in recent years had reached alarming numbers, the article said. The Magistrates had no control or regulation over these shops beyond seeing that under the local Police Act they were not kept open between midnight and five a.m. They had no control over their opening on Sundays, and the disorderly behaviour in these shops on the Sabbath was nothing short of a public scandal, it maintained. It was reported that young persons caroused in such premises, and girls had even been seen smoking there. There was neither necessity nor desire in Scotland for general Sunday trading, which, because of the extended operations of these foreign shopkeepers had developed to a very great extent in recent years, and the ice-cream trade functioned on that day to the serious detriment of the youth of the country. If a law on Sunday trading did no more than close those ice-cream parlours on that day it would be welcomed in Scotland as a great blessing. The Temperance Association went to law to enforce Sunday closure and was successful for a time.

These Italian immigrant owners of ice-cream parlours must have been surprised by the hostility they faced in the early years of such shops in Glasgow, since no such opposition had ever been shown to them as street vendors from ice-cream carts. In under 50 years, from 1860 to the early 1900s, by dint of hard work and initiative, some had progressed from street barrows and rudimentary shops in the slum districts to well appointed premises in the city centre, colourfully decorated, with mirrors on the walls and leather-covered seats set in secluded alcoves, where courting couples could eat their maccallums in privacy. For the conservatively-minded forces that controlled the city, already made anxious by the appearance of cinemas and dance halls, none of which of course were allowed to open on a Sunday, Italian ice-cream shops epitomized the evils of a decadence that was beginning to invade the hearts of the youth of Glasgow. The Italians were 'aliens' or foreigners who spoke a different language, they were purveyors of a luxurious and unnecessary commodity, ice-cream, and above all else, in a city run along strictly Presbyterian lines, they were Roman Catholics and traded on the Sabbath, the day of rest.

In one of his early novels, *Hatter's Castle*, A.J. Cronin reflects the attitudes of the day and gives us a glimpse of the genteel fear aroused by these shops in a certain section of the populace. The heroine, Mary, is taken by her lover Denis into an Italian café in Dumbarton:

> 'He took her arm firmly and led her a few doors down the street, then, before she realised it and could think even to resist, he had drawn her inside the cream-coloured doors of Bertorelli's café. She paled with apprehension, feeling that she had finally passed the limits of respectability, that the depth of her dissipation had now been reached, and looking reproachfully into Denis' smiling face, in a shocked tone she gasped:
>   "Oh, Denis, how could you?" '

Later in the narrative there comes this piece of erotic writing (by the standards of those days) which could well have put the book in the proscribed list together with *Lady Chatterley's Lover*.

> 'Now Mary was eating her macallum, a delicious concoction of ice-cream and raspberry juice, which, cunningly blending the subtly acid essence of the fruit with the cold mellow sweetness of the ice-cream, melted upon her tongue in an exquisite and unexpected delight. Under the table Denis pressed her foot gently with his, whilst his eyes followed her naïve enjoyment with a lively satisfaction.'

The *Glasgow Herald* on 6 May 1906 and on subsequent days carried a report on an attempt by the British Women's Temperance Association to ban the Sunday opening of these shops and to limit their hours on weekdays. The bright and inviting ice-cream parlours and the willingness of the Italians to work on Sundays had aroused the wrath of Glasgow's Sabbatarians. It was claimed by this organisation that the behaviour of customers in these shops was a public scandal and that this was because of the foreign traders whose influence had been to the detriment of the youth of the country. Evidence was given to the effect that boys and girls could be seen smoking cigarettes in these premises, and sometimes they could be seen dancing to the music of a harmonica! There was too much liberty given to the young, and cafés encouraged loose behaviour, they said. The city would be a far better place if they were all closed and all such activities banned, was their claim. The underlying theme in these attacks on ice-cream shops was that they were owned by 'aliens',★ and therefore had no place in British society.

The efforts of the Temperance Association gave rise to a a flow of letters to the editor of the *Glasgow Herald*, most of which were in favour of banning Sunday opening. One of these, by a Mr Drummond, made the assertion that: 'The ice-cream shops are perfect iniquities of hell itself and far worse than the evils of the Public House. They are sapping the morals of the youth of Scotland.'

To a large extent these attacks could be put down to xenophobia. Immigrants have always been faced with suspicion if not downright enmity from the local population, and the underlying theme of these criticisms was that the ice-cream shops were owned by 'aliens'. In one instance, in 1917, this became very clear in a case involving two Italian ice-cream shop owners in Paisley who had contravened the local shop-opening hours. According to the *Glasgow Herald*, at their trial Sheriff Blair, despite the fact that the charge against them was simply that of a contravention of local opening hours, saw fit to remark in his summation:

'These gentlemen seem to have no regard to the ordinary British methods of trading, and very little conception of what truth is. They put nothing in writing, they keep no books of any kind, they keep no bank accounts, they shelter behind their own ignorance real or assumed: they enter into so-called arrangements of partnership by which it is easy to defeat the claims of their British creditors, they buy and sell businesses on a plan that is unknown in this country, they juggle in and out of ownership like

★ In considering the phenomenon of xenophobia, it is perhaps worth reflecting on the fact that these foreigners of non-British extraction were known as 'aliens', a word of somewhat sinister extraterrestrial connotations, and not simply as 'foreigners', a word which does not evoke the same dark image. Yet I have never heard, for example, of an American classified as an 'alien' or even as a foreigner, for that matter, but always is spoken of as 'an American', and yet they are as 'alien' as an Italian under the law.

rabbits in a burrow, and then they quarrel amongst themselves and invoke the aid of our law.'

The coming of the Italians with their fish and chip and ice-cream shops was obviously not universally popular.

The opinions of the Paisley sheriff quoted above might well have been influenced by the activities of an old-time Glasgow Padrone, Mr Persichini, whose dress and appearance would not have been out of place in a gangster movie and who cocked a snoot regularly at the magistrates, a practice which obviously did not endear him to the authorities. Amongst other activities, he was the owner of a café at the corner of Union Street and Argyle Street, which opened every Sunday in contravention of the law. Religiously every Sunday the café would be visited by the police and Mr Persichini issued with a summons to appear the next day in front of the magistrate, and religiously every Monday morning he would be waiting at the court, there to pay with an ostentatious flourish his £2 fine. This procedure went on for years until the outbreak of the Second World War in 1939, at which time Mr Persichini was promptly arrested as an enemy alien and thus quite effectively put out of business.

Rumour had it in those days, rightly or wrongly, that Persichini was the driving force behind the notorious Rigardo house at Anderson Cross. Serafina Rigardo ran a notorious shebeen cum gambling house cum house of ill repute in Argyle Street at Anderston Cross. This house was open literally 24 hours a day for the purposes of drinking outwith permitted hours, for all sorts of gambling activities and for the supply of sexual favours. Although well and discreetly run for an establishment of its type, the constant stream of visitors and street cabs at all hours of the day and night gave rise to repeated complaints on the part of her neighbours, which resulted in a protracted police surveillance of the flat. It is not as easy as it may seem to prove that a house is being run as a shebeen. The fact that dozens of people are sitting around in a room quaffing whisky after whisky is not enough; they may, after all, be guests at a party and it must be shown that substantial amounts of liquor are stored on the premises and that money is being paid for the liquor consumed before action can be taken. Finally, after a protracted surveillance, a full-scale raid netted almost 50 gallons of alcohol in the form of spirits and wines on the premises. Serafina was nothing if not a patriot, for the police report mentions the wines as being 'Italian Chianti in straw-covered bottles'. Serafina was charged with 'trafficking in liquor without possessing a license', fined £100, and when it was discovered that she was an Italian citizen, immediately deported.

Once a shop had been opened, all the members of the owner's family were expected to help in the running of it. Generally speaking, with one or two enlightened exceptions of parents who could appreciate the opportunities offered by their new environment to their families, and who sacrificed themselves to give their children an education, the immigrant's family were expected to work behind the counter by the side of their father and mother. To be taught the family business, the children of many if not most Italian immigrants were taken away from school as soon as the school-leaving age of 14 was reached. This was my own case, as described in my book *Isle of the Displaced*, and in my working life I felt the same sense of dichotomy between my Scottish and Italian identities that I had found at school:

> 'There too the counter between myself and our customers acted as a barrier. We were aliens, foreigners, the Tallies who worked all day to serve them fish and chips and ice-cream, and we were tolerated as such.
>
> In retrospect, I suppose we were the Pakistani immigrants of our day, although in far lesser numbers, tolerated but not really accepted by the society in which we had chosen to make our homes. We were aliens who gave services to the community in the form of cafés and fish and chip shops which the locals themselves could not or would not provide, and we progressed by dint of long and hard hours of work. Integration was easier for us than it was for them, however. The colour of our skin was the same as that of our neighbours.'

It is difficult to imagine the culture-shock undergone by these early immigrants on arriving in a city like Glasgow at the end of the nineteenth and the beginning of the twentieth centuries. In the winter, Glasgow in those days was a city of fog and smog. There was many a day in the winter months when an impenetrable mixture of soot and mist would lie over the city, and a black darkness at noon prevailed. Possibly above all else, what would strike the immigrant, in addition to the soot-blackened tenements of the poorer areas where he almost certainly would have gone to live, would be the variety of smells and odours to assail his nostrils. Glasgow was then a city of smells which have now vanished from the city scene.

To take an example from one section of the city. At the northeast end of the Cowcaddens, apart from the omnipresent smell of coal fires in the winter, the immigrant's nostrils would be hit by the variety of smells emanating from the huge Buchanan Street railway goods station, with its vast stables to shelter the many scores of cart horses which hauled the heavy delivery carts. The air carried a mixture of steam, coal-dust and oil from the locomotives, together with a cocktail of smells from the crates and packages stacked on the platforms and loading areas. Mixed in with the stench from a fat-rendering works in Dobbies Loan there was the all pervading stink of a tannery in the same street. These smells would blend in with the distinctive subway odour which rose up from the Cowcaddens and Buchanan Street entries to the underground railway system.

From the tenement closes in which the immigrant now probably lived they would get a whiff of a typical slum tenement smell—a mixture of ripe backyard middens blended in with the smells from the common lavatories on each landing of the three-storey buildings. When the Italian immigrants began to open up their fish and chip shops, they themselves contributed in no small measure to the rich environmental stench. In those days there were no processed and odourless cooking oils such as there are now, and the fish and chip shops which were beginning to appear in substantial numbers fried their wares in pure dripping and lard. In the absence of modern filters and extraction systems, the smell so created, which led the fish and chip shops to be classified as a 'noxious trade', could wipe out all the other background smells of the area. In all, an environment further removed from the blue skies and clean air of their native land would be hard to imagine.

The immigrants too had their own environmental smells in their villages and towns of origin, but they were not to be compared to the smells caused by the industrial pollution of the Glasgow of 100 years ago. The tenement blocks of the working classes were built around the actual factories in which they worked, and the air around them was heavy with an assortment of industrial pollution. In the south side of the city, for example, until the late 1950s, the Govanhill district with its scores of tenements boasted of an iron-works with five blast furnaces. These furnaces, which were never extinguished, lit up the night sky and earned the area the name of Dixon's Blazes. With five huge chimneys spewing out fumes the atmosphere in the surrounding streets can be imagined. When my father first came to Glasgow from Barga in 1919 he found lodgings in Surrey Street in the Gorbals, at the northern side of Dixon's Blazes. Although he had worked in such places and worse outside of Italy before, the impact on my mother, who had never been out of sight of the Barga church tower in her life, was huge. But there were two factors in their new environment, bad as it was, which cancelled out all the negative ones: hope and opportunity.

These first immigrants to Scotland spoke little or no English, and when they did learn to communicate with the locals they were as often as not looked upon as figures of fun because of their distinct broken accent—note Adam McNaughtan's: 'you knew they were Tallies the minute they spoke'.

This image was taken up by the newly developing cinema industry, and one of the best known supporting actors in the films of the 20s and 30s was a little fat Italian, Henry Armetta, who despite having been born in America and speaking excellent English, or at least the American brand of it, made his fortune by his portrayal of the archetypal Italian immigrant and his funny fractured English.

All of the early immigrants, who always spoke amongst themselves in their native tongue even when a working knowledge of English had been acquired, had to adapt certain words for which there was no Italian equivalent. Pawnbrokers were unknown to them in Italy, so the word became *il Panbrocco*; loafer became *loffaro*. The word kettle, an article which did not exist in Italy, became *kettola*. The abuse they were often subjected to by the use of the four-letter F-word was described as *foccheggio*. They would very often continue with the use of these words when on visits to their home villages, much to the bewilderment of their relatives and friends.

H.L Mencken, in his book *The American Language,* a study of the impact of European languages on the development of language in America, quotes this extract from an New York Italian newspaper of the early 20s:

> 'I wuz inna barra Americana. La birra wuz Americana, Il padrone wuz Americano an dere was a ghenga di loffari Americani. Solo me wuz no Americano. I loffari say to me "Allo spaghetti man? You Americano man? Iu laico dis contri?" I say "No! no! Me Italiano man. No! No! Mi laico Italy."
>
> I loffari starta foccheggiare an starta fite, e mi noccarono out. When I wek up der wuz a polisseman say to me "Giroppe ya bomma!" an he arrest me!
>
> Nest day il gioggio say to me, "Wassa marra last naite?" an he fine me 10 dollari!'

In 1922, as Italy was beginning to develop as a nation, and with the coming to power of Mussolini and the Fascists, an attempt was made to draw the expatriate Italians scattered throughout Scotland closer together, and to give them a sense of pride and national unity. This sense of being Italian, rather than belonging to one particular region of that country, had slowly been taking root amongst the older generations of immigrants. These generations, who as young men had seen the unification of the various states that had gone to make up the Italian peninsula, had slowly acquired a sense of being Italian rather than of being Tuscan or Neapolitan or Sicilian, and this progress was accelerated during the First World War, when the people of the new Italian nation fought side by side against the common enemy, Germany.

An attempt had been made in London at the turn of the century to form a sort of trade union for Italians named *'La Societa' Di Mutuo Soccorso'* (Mutual Help Society) and a branch, largely ignored by the individualistic immigrants, was opened in Glasgow. After the First World War and the rise of Mussolini, the intensely nationalistic ethos of the fascist doctrine gave a further impetus to patriotic tendencies, and for the purpose of drawing expatriate immigrants closer together, a club known as *La Casa del Fascio* (Fascist House) was founded in Glasgow. In the early years of this organisation the members met in premises at the northern end of Renfield Street, which later were to form part of the Green's Playhouse cinema and dancehall complex.

Then in 1935 an Italian consulate was established in Glasgow. This was housed in a magnificent building in Park Circus designed by the architect Charles Wilson at the end of the 1880s, and is reckoned to be his finest achievement. The mansion, with its columned entrance hall and rich plasterwork, was in a bad state of disrepair and was purchased through public contributions from within the Scottish Italian community, which by now was achieving a considerable measure of financial success. The necessary repairs and decoration were carried out by the skilled labourers and artists who were now beginning to make an appearance amongst the immigrants, and the activities of the *Casa del Fascio* were transferred to the new quarters in Park Circus. The *Casa del Fascio* (which after the war dropped the word *Fascio* and became *Casa d'Italia*) acted in the main as a meeting point for all Italians living in Scotland, a place where they could socialise and meet regularly. The main aims of the old *Casa del Fascio* were to provide a social club for the Italian community, to conduct Italian language classes for children born in Scotland who had no knowledge of their parents' native tongue and to encourage and foster an interest in the Italian language and culture. The Casa also organised trips to Italy for the younger Italians, where they could participate in so-called *Balilla* camps, a type of military boy scout organisation which was run along military lines, with the boys dressed in black uniforms and drilling with toy guns.

Unfortunately, all this did not go to better the image that many Scots had of the Italians who had come to live amongst them, and, rightly or wrongly, the impression was being created that the Italians were attempting to set up a local fascist political party. The rise of fascism in Europe and the British version of it under Oswald Mosley had created many bitter political tensions, even amongst the British, and to many of them *La Casa del Fascio* represented the embodiment of a system which ran counter to their political values. This feeling came to a head at the time of the Italian invasion of Ethiopia, when economic sanctions were imposed against Italy. To help counter these sanctions the Italian government asked all Italians abroad to send back any gold objects—rings, bracelets, ear-rings, gold ornaments of any kind—as a gift to the State, and the consulate in Glasgow acted as a gathering centre. The rise of a degree of anti-Italian sentiment motivated a handful of Italians in Glasgow to change their names to Anglo-Saxon ones, so as not to be known as Italians. Fernando Nobile became Freddie Noble, Luigi Mastrocoia became Louie Masters, and one of the Di Ciacca brothers of Glasgow assumed the surname Everest. This created a deal of anger in the families concerned, the argument being that somehow their parentage was being betrayed.

The rise of fascism in Italy also served to create tensions within the Italian community here, for there were many whose political opinions ran counter to the beliefs and aims of the new government of Mussolini. Many of the older generation were intensely socialistic and individualistic in their outlook and had never looked favourably on the founding of *La Casa Del Fascio* and refused to have anything to do with its activities. Those who criticised the actions of Mussolini, and they were many, were labelled as anti-Italian by their fellows, and the post-fishmarket meetings in Cooper's coffee house often ended in an acrimonious exchange of insults. These became particularly bitter at the time of the murder of the left-wing journalist Matteotti by the fascists in Rome, and on one occasion the management of Coopers threatened to bar all Italians unless these political arguments ceased. Despite all these internal tensions and despite the unemployment and economic depression of that era, during the 20s and the 30s, most Italians began to prosper and to achieve a degree of affluence. The most enterprising who had struck out on their own and who had seized whatever opportunities had come their way were now beginning to reap substantial rewards for their hard work. They continued to bring over new immigrants as workers and to expand their enterprises, and many, as a result of their economical life style, had by now accumulated enough money to achieve the dream of returning home to Italy as prosperous men and women. Their return, of course, served as a further incentive for others to try to follow in their footsteps. The Italian colony in Glasgow had slowly begun to climb the social and professional ladder; street pedlars had become the owners of little cafés and fish and chip shops, waiters had now acquired the ownership of their own restaurants, and parents could now see the dawn of a new and prosperous future for themselves and for their children.

🎔 6 🎔

The 1920s and 1930s

By the end of the 1920s and throughout the 1930s the status of the little Italian community in Scotland had radically altered. Many of them, who had been street vendors of ice-cream in the summer and roasted chestnuts in winter, had by now, as described in the previous chapter, become the owners of cafés and fish and chip shops and had become relatively affluent. They had worked hard and long, they had provided services and value for money hitherto unknown to the native Scots, and many of their sons could now take advantage of their new prosperity and make use of the opportunities offered by the Scottish educational system. Their unsophisticated and sometimes only semi-literate parents, denied the chance of an education by the poverty and by the rigid class system they had come away from, began to dream that their offspring could one day become doctors or teachers or lawyers, and as the grinding weight of poverty slowly lifted from their shoulders, they became less and less demanding that their children should work behind the counter in the family shop rather than continue in education. It was not that every immigrant's child aspired to academic success. Far from it. There is nothing like a full wallet to inspire confidence, and ambition and the money that was beginning to pour into the shop-tills fuelled the desire of their sons to do bigger and better things in business.

Those years were something of a golden era for the Italians in Scotland. It was in these two decades, after a generation of setting down roots, that the community achieved a degree of stability and an increasing economic prosperity. They began to make a place for themselves in society and became gradually more and more accepted by the people among whom they had chosen to live. The immigrants were ambitious entrepreneurs, albeit mainly on a small scale. They were for the most part self-employed, and in their little shops they created jobs for the locals at a time when Britain was undergoing a great economic depression with unemployment running into the millions. However, in this period legal restrictions at both ends of the chain of migration began to make themselves felt. In 1920 an Aliens Order was passed by Parliament, and instead of the free entry which had been available to immigrants from all countries, this act now placed obstacles for those wishing to enter the UK, so that only foreigners who had been able to obtain work permits could now come here to take up residence. For those who wanted to do so, a work permit could only be secured if the migrant had someone in Britain prepared to make the necessary application to the Ministry of Labour, and it had to be shown that the job on offer could not be filled by a native of the country. Secondly, in Italy a new fascist government had come to power in the early 1920s. Mussolini, as other leaders of the newly born Italian state before him had been, was aware that the steady stream of so many young, fit and ambitious men and women flowing out of the country was denuding Italy of its best brains and manpower. So depleted had Italy become of young able-bodied men that at the beginning of the First World War she was incapable of raising an army, and had to mount recruitment campaigns in the USA and in South America amongst Italian immigrants there. To stop this haemorrhage of valuable humanity, severe anti-emigration laws were passed by the new fascist government and generous government grants were given to those Italians prepared to raise large families.

Despite all the obstacles to be overcome, a few Italians did succeed in entering Britain during this period, and those who came to Scotland did so mainly to work in cafés and fish and chip shops already established there, and on work permits applied for by the owners of these businesses, who were usually relatives. These new immigrants, individualistic as always, after having served out their indenture and apprenticeship, as it were, in due time set up their own small businesses, with cafés and fish and chip shops predominating. A few, skilled in other crafts such as mosaic and terrazzo work, also set up their own workshops, and south of the border in the large population centres this type of work was almost exclusively carried out by Italians. A sense of security and expectation of future prosperity now permeated the Italian community. A way of life which enabled ambitious parents to raise and support a family and offered everyone willing to work hard a prosperity and security unknown in Italy had been found. The future was full of hope for the young and the ambitious Scots-Italian.

Some Italian names had by this time become famous in Scotland for the excellence of their products and services. In the west of Scotland the Nardini and the Castelvecchi families of Largs had acquired an outstanding reputation in catering for the needs of the day trippers and holidaymakers who, before the arrival of the cheap and attractive Spanish package holidays, flocked to the Clyde resorts in their thousands. Their café restaurants, attractively fitted out in the glittering Art Deco style of the thirties, did a roaring trade at their respective ends of the Largs promenade. Indeed, it could be said that the ever-growing prosperity of the town of Largs as a whole was based on the existence of these two rival catering establishments. They acted as a magnet to the Glasgow day-tripper and holidaymaker who wanted to spend some time 'Doon the Watter' and indulge himself with an upmarket fish tea or an enticingly presented maccallum.

Every resort on the Firth of Clyde, from Rothesay to Girvan, had fine beaches and beautiful vistas of the sea to offer the holidaymaker, but none of these resorts could even begin to compete with what Largs had to give in the way of catering facilities. These were epitomised by the Nardini and Castelvecchi cafés, which not only served excellent ice-cream and fish suppers, but were also ideal as a place to shelter pleasantly from the very often inclement summer weather. There is nothing more miserable than to spend a holiday in a cold and rain-swept seaside resort with very little to offer in the way of shelter and entertainment, but the Moorings, as the Castelvecchi café was known, and Nardini's offered a pleasant haven for families to while away the time when the weather did not permit of outdoor activities, a frequent occurrence during the unpredictable Scottish summers.

Every Clyde coast resort was well supplied with ice-cream shops. Amongst scores of other cafés in these seaside towns, Rothesay had the Zavaroni café, especially well known through Lena Zavaroni of the lovely singing voice, whose life was to end tragically because of the ravages of anorexia. Gourock had its Biagioni café and Ardrossan the Cavani café, Troon had its Togneri café, known locally as Tog's place, and Irvine had the Corrieri café. Prestwick had the Lake Café at Prestwick Cross, owned by the internationally known footballer of the thirties, Johnny Moscardini. Johnny was born in Falkirk a few months after his parents' arrival in this country, and grew up and was educated there. A first class footballer, he played for Falkirk for a spell, then in the early twenties spent some years in Italy. He played for the Italian national team which won the World Cup in Czechoslovakia in 1934, then returned to Scotland to help his father run the newly opened Lake Café at Prestwick Cross. Apart from the fact that he ran a first class combination ice-cream café and fish and chip shop, Johnny had friends in high places at the Old Prestwick Golf Club, and could always manage to get a round on those hallowed links for his friends, which was a rare treat at a time when golf for those young Italians who had become enamoured of the game was confined to playing the crowded local municipal courses. Johnny escaped military service in the British Army during the war by dint of the fact that he had a withered left arm, which obviously had not been a drawback to his football ability.

None of these relatively small shops could be compared to either Nardini's or the Moorings. In size alone these two were much larger than all of the above named put together. They seated customers in their many hundreds, as opposed to the ten or twenty tables available in most cafés, and did so in spacious and luxurious style. Moreover, their menu was far more extensive and varied than was on offer anywhere else, and their position, at opposite ends of the busy Largs promenade, was ideal for the strollers who were seized by the urge to sit down to some exotic ice-cream concoction or, when the weather permitted, to buy an ice-cream cone and lick it as they sauntered along the Prom. Live music was provided by the two cafés at weekends, creating an atmosphere akin to the Albert Sandler Palm Court broadcasts of the wireless era. The Moorings had a dance floor on the top storey of the building and weekend bus runs from Glasgow included tickets for 'the dancing' there. The intense and sometimes bitter rivalry between the two families in providing amenities and quality for their customers went to the benefit of the trippers who patronised them.

The Nardini family came to Largs in the early 30s from Paisley, where they had successfully established themselves in a café and fish and chip business, but the Castelvecchi clan had come directly to Largs at the turn of the century, where the story of their career could serve as a blueprint in the history of the economic development of the Italian immigrant. They came from Barga, the picturesque little hilltop town in the hills near Lucca, as did the Nardinis, and set up a little ice-cream café in an old ramshackle building directly on the corner facing the pier. This was probably the best site for such a trade anywhere in Largs, since every passenger embarking or disembarking on any of the ferryboats plying up and down the Clyde had to pass their door. Small though the shop was, they did a roaring trade in ice-cream in the summer, and a brisk trade all year round with the sale of sweets, chocolates and cigarettes.

During the winter months the three Castelvecchi brothers worked hard at putting in a stock of ice for the manufacture of ice-cream in the summer. In the cold days of hard frost they would make their way with a horse and cart to the top of the winding Haylie Brae and the many frozen pools of water to be found in the open fields. They would fill the cart with ice, which would then be taken down to a large cellar deep under their shop. Lined with layer upon layer of straw, with a bedding of sawdust to help in the insulation, this cellar served as an ice-well, where the ice could remain for months without melting and could be used in the summer for the manufacture of ice-cream. The pieces of ice were carefully stacked, and the cellar was well drained so that water would not accumulate and melt the ice. Although artificial means had been developed in America for producing ice in factories as many as 30 years before by a man called Jarman, and although an ice factory had been operative in Glasgow since the early twenties, the 'artificial' ice so produced was expensive, and since the Haylie Brae source cost nothing except their hard work, this helped to swell the profits of the café from the sale of ice-cream.

The Castelvecchi brothers were ambitious and far-seeing, and slowly over the years had acquired the ownership of all the little shops in the block around them, and the whole site came under their control. At the beginning of the 1930s, with help and guidance of their local bank manager, a loan of the staggering sum of £30,000 was obtained, and with this an imposing three-storied café restaurant with dancehall was built on the site of their original little corner café. The new building was designed with the corner facing the sea slightly curved upwards, to give the impression of the prow of a ship and thus became known as the Moorings. £30,000 is nothing these days, but to put the sum in perspective, in the early thirties a London Italian, Primo Scala, won that same sum in the Irish Sweepstakes and became a seven day wonder. For weeks on end the national newspapers ran headlines with stories about the colossal fortune won by a London terrazzo worker.

News of this vast loan percolated down through the Italian community and prophecies of doom, gloom and bankruptcy were made over the interminable cups of coffee sipped each morning by the side of the roaring open fire at Cooper's café in Howard Street. Never had anyone been so wrong. The Moorings was a colossal success and established the Castelvecchi family's enduring fortune. On the death of the last of the founder brothers some 25 years or so ago, the Moorings was sold to a firm of property developers, the café and restaurant were demolished and a luxury apartment block with the same name stands there now.

The financial and political power exercised in Largs by the Castelvecchi family in their heyday was considerable. In the 1970s they applied for planning permission to convert the tenement which stood next to the café, and which they had been using to house their staff, into a public house and bar. The application was opposed by a local temperance society and refused by the licensing authority. The family immediately took out a two-page advert in the local paper listing all their properties and business activities in the town and their contributions in local rates to the township of Largs, plus a list of all the local workers, as opposed to Italians, employed by them. The list of workers ran into several hundreds, and the amount of rates paid ran into many hundreds of thousands of pounds. The family asked if it was just and proper that a company which provided so many jobs, contributed such huge amounts in rates to the town and attracted such substantial revenue to it, should be refused the opportunity to further benefit the community financially simply because of the objection of some obscure temperance society. The story was taken up by the national press, and at the next meeting of the licensing court the application was unanimously granted.

The Nardinis in Paisley had observed these early developments with interest, and, in the early 1930s, spurred on by the success of the Moorings, they in their turn bought an old house and a piece of land about 400 yards along the prom and proceeded to build an Art Deco café-restaurant complex there. The café was the largest in Britain, had some of the finest Art Deco furnishings of the time and boasted the first ever American-style soda fountain in the UK. During the war the Nardinis were interned on the Isle of Man, but returned to their business at the end of hostilities. They prospered until well into the 1980s, when cheap charter flights began to attract holidaymakers to the sunnier climes of the Mediterranean, where the weather was as good as guaranteed and the prices very much lower. In the face of this new and unmatchable competition, the attraction of Largs and other Clyde resorts for the Glasgow holidaymaker faded, and the roaring trade once done by the café slowed down very considerably. Later still, after the death of the founder brothers, acrimonious family differences forced the sale of the business and gave rise to a change of ownership. The café exists to this day, unchanged in its external appearance, and still trades under the Nardini name.

A touch of irony to the intense rivalry between the Nardinis and the Castelvecchis has entered into the story of the two families. Roberto Nardini, son of one of the founders, was ousted from the Nardini company at the time of the family differences. He promptly acquired the corner unit at the new Moorings apartment building, fitted it out as a café, and trades there as the Café Nardini. The three Castelvecchi brothers must have shifted slightly in their grave at the thought that the son of one of their arch-rivals was now trading on what had been their territory. The new owners of the original Nardini complex went to court in a failed attempt to prevent the use of the name Nardini by Roberto in his new café.

The two families were large importers of labour from their native Barga district, and the Castelvecchis bought a small tenement block at the side of the restaurant for the housing of their immigrant labour. In both cafés the important positions in the kitchens and all cash points were usually manned by Italians, whilst the staff in direct contact with the public were in the main all locally recruited. The immigrant workers were well trained by the two companies, and therefore much sought after by other Italian employers, with the result that many of them were poached by Glasgow restaurant and café owners and lured away from Largs by the offer of larger wages. Over the years score upon score of workers from Barga served their apprenticeship in the Nardini and Castelvecchi cafés, and now every year a festa, *'La Sagra del Pesce e Patate'* (the Fish and Chip Festival) is celebrated by them and their descendants in that little Tuscan town. Fish and chip ranges are set up in the town square and the retired fish friers of Barga, all of them with their trade learned in Scotland and many from Largs, vie with one another to produce the perfect fish supper for the tourists who now flock in their thousands to the picturesque town.

The success of the Largs Italians had been mirrored, although on a much smaller scale, in Glasgow and Edinburgh. The ice-cream barrows that once had plied the streets of the two cities had soon been discarded, to be replaced by luxuriously appointed cafés, and the purely functional fish and chip shops to be found everywhere had been transformed into bright and attractive places where people would flock to partake of a fish tea or some such snack before a night at the 'Pictures' or a visit to one of the many theatres which dotted the centre of Glasgow.

At one end of the catering spectrum in Glasgow there was Ferrari's restaurant at 10 Sauchiehall Street, with cuisine to match anything London had to offer. Slightly downmarket from Ferrari's you had the Berkeley at Charing Cross owned by the Equi family, luxuriously appointed but with a much simpler and popularly priced menu. At the other end of the spectrum there was the Savoy in Renfrew Street, an unpretentious down-to-earth fish and chip shop owned by our own family, which served fish teas, reckoned by some to be the best in town, by the hundreds to the city centre cinema and theatre-going population of Glasgow. Close by in Parliamentary Road stood the San Remo fish and chip shop, owned by one of the original immigrants to Glasgow, Carlo Gennasi, and run by his protégé Gino Ferretti. The San Remo was probably the busiest chip shop in Glasgow and went through an unbelievable amount of fish and chips. On its busiest day, a Saturday, as opposed to the Friday of most other chip shops, it was not unknown for it to go through 20 one hundredweight bags of potatoes—one ton of chips!—and 18 boxes of fish, with each box containing about 2½ to 3 stone of unfilleted fish. And all this business done in a little shop that could fit into a very small corner of a modern Harry Ramsden's. Apart from being the busiest, it was without a doubt the roughest and most difficult to run in the entire city. A few yards away from the Killermont Street bus station and surrounded by a variety of drinking dens and shebeens, never a night went by but what disturbances and fights took place there, all of which were handled swiftly, efficiently and mercilessly by the hard-as-nails Gino Ferretti.

In between these, dotted all over the city's various districts, there were scores of good quality ice-cream shops and fish restaurants, all highly profitable and all owned by Italian immigrant families, with the father of the family as like as not having started his career by pushing an ice-cream barrow along a Glasgow street. Names like Coia, Rossi, Di Ciacca, Crolla, Risi, Conetta, Guidi, Gennasi, Biagi, Pacitti, De Marco, all became well known to Glaswegians through the quality of the various services they had to offer in their ice-cream and fish and chip shops. The Coia clan was especially prolific. With origins in the Filignano district of the south of Italy, the first Coias had come to Scotland in the late nineteenth century and had set roots down in practically every town and city in the land. The name Coia is said to derive from Goya, a common name amongst the Spaniards who for many decades had ruled over that part of Italy. The scale of the exodus of the Coia clan from the Filignano area to Scotland can be seen from the following statistic: at the time of writing, there are more than 91 Coias in the Glasgow phone book, with probably several more ex-directory. In the phone directory of Rome, now a city of some two million inhabitants, there are exactly nine! It is safe to say that there is not a town of any size in Scotland which does not have a Coia amongst its inhabitants.

One of the Coias, Vincent, established a bakery in the Garscube Road district, where his VC pies were in great demand. Vincent had the hot pie concession at Firhill, the Partick Thistle football ground in Maryhill. Half-time at all Glasgow football grounds saw a great consumption of hot pies by the fans and the pie concession at these venues was much sought after. The pie-eating public at Firhill were blissfully unaware that the initials VC stood for Vincent Coia, and not for Victoria Cross as everyone imagined. The Renucci family of Dalmally Lane in Maryhill with their Kelvindale bakery were great business rivals of his, with a city-wide distribution of their particular brand of meat pie. There was Peter Coia, now into his eighties and still fit enough to play golf three times a week, whose café near the Southern General Hospital had the biggest sale of Terry's chocolate boxes of any confectioners in Glasgow. Had he been so minded, Peter Coia could have made a fortune in the restaurant business. His wife Anna, who for 15 years served the community by means of her voluntary work in the Citizen's Advice Bureau, is a wonderful cook who despite the advancing years still enjoys entertaining their many friends, and had she so wished her talent could have been commercially developed.

Then there was Jack Coia the architect, with half a dozen titles after his name and designer and builder of exotic church structures which were not always to the liking of conservatively minded congregations. His church in East Kilbride was given the name 'St Fort Apache' by the parishioners, because of its grim forbidding exterior. Jack Coia was the son of an organ grinder, who in 1898 together with his wife walked and ground their organ all the way from Filignano in the Abruzzi hills to Scotland, with their infant son in a basket on the barrel organ. Following arrival in Glagow they eventually opened a café in the Parkhead district, where they prospered enough to be able to have their son Jack educated at St Aloysius college, then to go on to the Glasgow School of Architecture. Then there was Emilio Coia the artist, whose paintings and sketches were much sought after.

Leaving these last two Coias aside, perhaps the best known Coia in Scotland is Dave, now very much nearer 90 than 80, but still as fit and as active as many a man 20 years his junior. Dave Coia's grandfather came to Scotland in 1885, and made his living by pushing an ice-cream cart along the streets of Wranghom, later to be named New Stevenson. Five years later, in 1890, Dave's father was born, by which time the ice-cream barrow had given way to a little ice-cream shop. Dave, himself saw the light of day in a tenement flat by the side of the shop in 1914, and began his career there at the age of fourteen, serving ice-cream wafers over the counter. The long and restrictive hours of café life did not suit well with Dave and it was not long until he sought a change in his line of work. A friend of his, a well-known Motherwell footballer of the day named Johnny Murdoch, worked for the Clydesdale tube works, which in the early 30s were transferred south to Corby in Lincolnshire. John Murdoch went south with his firm, and some time later Dave decided to put café work behind him and found a job beside his friend in the newly transferred tube factory. Although a definite change from café work, this was hardly an occupation that would have lead to a fortune, so he returned north once more, married his wife Bruna and raised the cash to set up a fish and chip shop in Kirkintilloch. Even in his marriage Dave showed his independence and individuality. Bruna was born in Barga, and Dave's family came from the province of Frosinone in the South. There is an Italian proverb, to the effect that if you are looking for a successful marriage you should pick someone born in your own street. It was expected in Italian families in those days that one should marry one's own kind from one's own district, and it is a measure of the outlook of the times that the respective families of Bruna and Dave frowned upon what they considered to be akin to a union of foreigners.

Through profitable, life in a fish and chip shop was every bit as claustrophobic as café life had been, but Dave was rescued from it by the outbreak of war, when he was given a uniform and served for four years in a transport unit of the Army. The war over, he turned his back on fish and chips and took up the shopfitting trade with great success and there is still many a café and lounge bar in Glasgow beautifully designed and fitted out by his company. On one occasion he took up the role of impresario, bringing to a hall in Kirkcaldy a young and as yet unknown group from Liverpool who went by the improbable name of the Beatles. From shopfitting he branched out into the juke-box leasing business, which developed into the leasing of gaming machines, and now, trading under the name of Rallin Ltd., Dave with his two sons Ronnie and Adrian preside over the biggest company of its type in Scotland. Every time a coin is inserted into a pinball or fruit machine in any club or pub in Scotland, very probably that machine belongs to Dave and his group. The list of notable Coias could go on and on. There is even a James Giulio Coia from Shettleston who served as chief engineer during the war on Lord Mountbatten's flagship *Windsor Castle*.

Not all Italians followed the fish and chip and ice-cream road to success. A handful established themselves as barbers and hairdressers, and it was not long before the Glasgow public were queuing up to have their tonsorial needs attended to by a Vezza, or a Camillo, a Di Fazio, a Pediani, a Liverani or a a Di Tano. Marcello Di Tano, long retired and now well into his seventies, contributed much to the social life of the Scottish Italians and continues to do so through his Laziale Club. Marcello organises dances in St Thomas' church hall in Riddrie in the winter months, and tickets for these occasions are at a premium. Although all age groups are catered for, traditional Italian music dominates the evening, and the older members of the audience steep themselves in the nostalgia of the music and songs. Marcello was one who saw to it that his family should receive the education that he was denied, and his son Armando now occupies an important position in an internationally known electronics firm.

The Toffolo family, terrazzo workers from the Friuli Venezia Giulia district in the extreme north-east of Italy, founded the Toffolo-Jackson terrazzo and mosaic factory, which was to become famous throughout Scotland. Louis

Toffolo, one of the founders, was the grandfather of Joe Zangrande, retired lecturer in the Glasgow College of Building, who had a narrow escape from being interned at the outbreak of war. Joe was born in Glasgow in 1925, but spent the years between the age of 5 and 9 in Italy, where he received his first schooling. He returned to Glasgow at the age of 10, and his father enrolled him in the Casa del Fascio as a member of the *Balilla*, the fascist equivalent of the Boy's Brigade. As a member of that group his name appeared in the list of persons to be arrested on 10 June 1940. He was 14 at the time, and his distraught mother had to produce his birth certificate to the arresting officers as proof that he fell outside the age category of those to be interned, and that his name should not have been on their list. Later in the war he joined the Highland Light Infantry, with which he saw action for a few months at the end of the war.

The name Catani became famous for shopfitting through the business started up by Oscar, the elder of two brothers from the town of San Marcello Pistoiese, a few kilometres from Barga. The three Fazzi brothers, also from the Barga area, were the first to establish an Italian delicatessen in the west of Scotland. Their shop in Clyde Street, near the fish market, became a Mecca for all Italians who sought foods imported from the homeland, and their name became synonymous with fine Italian wines and delicatessen. They were followed in the same line of business by the Da Prato family in an attempt to rival them as Italian warehousemen. Sandro Sarti, who came from Barga to help manage the Fazzi business, married one of the Fazzi daughters and now runs a chain of successful Italian restaurants of his own in Glasgow.

The Risi brothers, Albert and Ernie, also broke away from their café connections, which had been established many years before by their father, Angelo. Risi senior was one of the early immigrants and had arrived in Glasgow from Cervaro in the province of Frosinone at the end of the nineteenth century. He made his living, as most other Italians did, by selling ice-cream in the streets of the city, then, having saved his pennies, and with the help of his young family, opened his own small café in London Road near Bridgeton Cross.

The last days of Angelo Risi give an interesting insight into some of the difficulties faced by early immigrants in moments of crisis because of their rudimentary knowledge of the language. Angelo became ill and was taken to the Royal Infirmary, where, under the stress of his illness, he forgot the little English he knew and was no longer able to communicate. A local café owner, a Mr Tartaglia, had to be summoned to translate for him. Angelo knew he was dying, and the Italian consul of the day had to be called in to take down the dying man's spoken will. Angelo had to be identified to the consul by two persons, and his dying wishes were written down. A translation then had to be attested to by a Glasgow lawyer so that Angelo Risi's last wishes could be implemented.

Ernie Risi had worked for a spell with the three Fazzi brothers, and because of the increasing prosperity of the Italian colony he realized the potential trade that was there to be done in Italian imports of that nature. The potential lay not only in the Italian community, for by now the Scots were becoming ever more sophisticated in their eating habits, and they too wanted to taste the delights of Italian fare. The two brothers set up their own delicatessen business in Stockwell Street across from the fish market. Albert, who is now well into his eighties, travelled the length and breadth of Scotland as a salesman for his business, and is a walking encyclopaedia of the names and connections of Scottish-Italian families. He is fond of reminiscing about the past, as all elderly men are, and now gives thanks for the discrimination against Italians, or all aliens, for that matter, prevalent in Scottish society in those early days. Anxious to break away from the drudgery in the family ice-cream shop, as a youth he had taken a course at Skerry's further education college so as to be able to apply for a civil service job at the end of it. His diploma acquired, on applying for a post he was informed that, because of his Italian parentage, even though he was British-born, all government jobs were closed to him, even that of a postman. For which he now gives heartfelt thanks, for he then was forced to embark on what was to be a very prosperous and lucrative business career.

The name Pacitti also takes up a fair amount of space in the Glasgow phone book. There are 25 Pacittis listed, a good number of them descended from what were called the Russian Pacittis by the Italian colony, so as to differentiate them from those who had come directly from Italy. The grandfather of Gina Pacitti, founder of the law firm of Pacitti-Jones, was born in Russia. His parents had gone there from a little village called Pietrafitta near Monte Cassino to sell embroidered lace and they lived and worked in Petrograd for a number of years. For some reason or other they decided to come to Scotland and they arrived in Portobello in 1920 just a few weeks before Gina's father Charlie was born. In the early thirties they came to Glasgow, where Charlie eventually set up a mini-supermarket, 'Pacitti's of Burnside', which became a landmark in the Rutherglen-Burnside district. Charlie, who died some years ago, spoke a unique brand of Italian. His was the local Pietrafitta dialect, which he spoke with a toothless Russian accent, acquired from his mother, who had no teeth and had picked up a Russian accent during her years in Petrograd. Charlie, like many of these immigrant parents with little or no education, saw to it that his family made full use of their potential. His daughter Gina, graduate in Law from Glasgow University, has five law and estate agent offices in the Glasgow area, and of his three sons, the eldest Nicky lectures in English at Pisa University, the second son Eric became head of the Middle Eastern division of Rothman's tobacco company by reason of his PhD in Arabic and business management, and Mark, the youngest, has his own accountancy firm in London.

Eliseo Moscardini from Barga, owner of a little fish and chip shop in Maryhill Road, had the satisfaction of seeing his son Tino become one of the first Italian lawyers in Glasgow. This was a satisfaction shared by Ottavio Franchi, who from a little fish and chip shop at the top of the Butney Brae in Maryhill saw his son Oswaldo graduate in law at Glasgow university. Oswaldo founded his own law firm and then went on to become the Italian Consul in Glasgow. His son Leandro also chose law as a career, also has his own law firm and holds the post of Italian Vice Consul in Glasgow. The Consulate was transferred to offices in Edinburgh some years ago, a strange decision, given that the bulk of Italians in Scotland live in Glasgow and the west of Scotland.

The ice-cream family Colpi from Milngavie saw their daughter become a successful writer, as did the Di Mambros from Motherwell, whose daughter Anne is a prolific writer of TV drama scripts. Anne's father survived the war as an internee in Camp 43 on St Helene's Island at Montreal, where he was transported on the prison ship *Ettrick* in 1940. My brother Ralph and myself, who both left school at the age of 14 to work in the family shop, have seen all of our children graduate from university. Ralph, who sadly died some months ago in his 93rd year, would have been justly proud of his son Frank, a lawyer advocate who has just been appointed Sheriff to the district of South Strathclyde. Frank's wife Dorothy runs a successful law office in Glasgow, Pieri-Graham. Ralph has two more daughters, Viviana and Maria, the latter of whom has just retired as schoolteacher. I, myself, can look with a degree of satisfaction at a consultant psychiatrist son, and three daughter university graduates, one with a BSC from Glasgow University, one a lawyer, and one who lectures in English at the University of Pisa. It is worth mentioning that whilst I was admiring the view through the barbed wire in Canada as an internee, Ralph was busy serving for four years in the British Army.

The list of professional people whose education was paid for by the profits made from the sale of ice-cream and fish and chips and by the hard work and sweat of their largely uneducated parents is long. Marcella Evaristi, writer, is the daughter of Louie, owner of café and fish and chip shops. Frank Pignatelli, head of Glasgow Education Department, is the son of a café proprietor. Dr Abrami, noted orthopaedic surgeon, was the son of a fish and chip shop owner; whilst Sir Eduardo Paolozzi, the world famous sculptor, who was awarded the OBE in 1968 and knighted in 1988, lost his Edinburgh café owner father in the sinking of the *Arandora Star*. Prominent amongst these names is that of Richard Demarco OBE, one of the founders of the Traverse Theatre in Edinburgh, famous as an actor, artist and lecturer; and last but by no means least there is the Archbishop of Glasgow, Mario Conti, born in Elgin to parents who came to Scotland from Barga.

Some who had benefited from their parents' wish that they be educated, and who had acquired university degrees, did not continue with a professional career, however. Having seen the money there was to be made in the shops set up by their immigrant fathers, they chose to continue in that sphere, where, no matter how unpleasant the work, the material benefits were far greater than ever could be earned in any of the professions. A case in point is that of Romy Di Mascio of Glasgow who, despite a degree from Glasgow University, decided to return to the family café business after the war. A wise decision financially, for he now commands a chain of properties throughout the city.

To return to the Coias. Not all of them were law-abiding citizens. Goldie Coia was a remarkable man with a great deal of talent, who could have achieved much had he kept to the straight and narrow. He was brought up in Belshill where his father ran an ice-cream shop. There, as a boy, he was involved in a tragic accident which the psychologists now would probably say had a bearing on the life of crime which he chose to follow. When about ten years of age, he was on a visit with his parents to his uncle and in a desk drawer he discovered what he thought was a toy pistol. He pointed it at his uncle in jest, pulled the trigger and killed him with a bullet in the eye. What the boy thought was a toy was in fact an only too real and fully-loaded automatic pistol.

In his late teens Goldie embarked on a life of fraud and crime, his first exploit being the hold-up of a bank in Renfield Street in the late thirties. He walked into the premises and pointed a napkin-covered finger at a teller and demanded money. The teller had no way of knowing that there was no gun under the napkin, only a finger, so he duly handed over a bundle of banknotes. With his newly gained wealth, Goldie went to the downstairs washrooms in the Central Station, treated himself to a haircut and a shoe-shine and tipped the boy £5! That was much more than a week's wages then, and the bemused shoe-shine boy went immediately round the corner to the Horseshoe Bar in

Drury Lane and stood everybody there drinks. This very unusual largesse filtered down to the attention of the police, who had no difficulty in tracing it back to Goldie, who got a jail sentence for his pains. The sentence was short because of the skill of Goldie's lawyer, who in the trial established the fact that no threat had been made, no weapon had been involved, and that Goldie had simply pointed a cloth-covered finger at the teller and had asked him for money.

On his release he never looked back, and embarked on a lifetime career of fraud and deceit in nearly every country in Europe, spending a fair amount of time in their jails. He never again, however, used the implied threat of violence in his escapades. His death some years ago was the occasion of an article in the Glasgow *Daily Record*, which gave a brief resumé of some of his more spectacular exploits. Once, with the help of some friends in the crew of the *Queen Mary*, which was at the time on a regular transatlantic route, he smuggled himself aboard the liner and hid in the crew's quarters. He emerged each day to circulate with the paying passengers and became one of the best known faces in the first class section. At the end of the journey he was several hundred pounds the richer, money legitimately won from passengers at the card tables. His deception was uncovered on arrival in the USA by the immigration authorities, and he was immediately shipped back to the UK in the same liner, this time well under guard in steerage. At the time of his death he was negotiating with the *Daily Record* for the right to write the story of his life of crime. At the beginning of Goldie's career in crime a deportation order was made against him, but that failed, since he was British-born.

Another who did not take to the shop life of his parents was Victor Russo, son of a Coatbridge café owner. Besotted by a diet of early James Cagney and Edward G. Robinson gangster movies, he took to dressing like the Hollywood idea of a gangster and carried a gun in a holster under his arm, although there is no record of him ever having used it. He went to London to offer his services to the infamous Kray Brothers. Nothing is known of his short stay there, but on his return to Glasgow he became something of a caricature. The records show that he was arrested 6 times in 8 days for disorderly behaviour. As in the case of Goldie Coia, a deportation order was made against him, but that failed also, given that Victor too was British-born.

Another Italian bad egg of the day was a street bookie by the name of Tony Biagi, or Biaj as he was known to the locals, who used his betting pitch off the Garscube Road for the resetting of stolen goods. The place was raided by the police and a mass of stolen goods discovered. The raid resulted in Tony Biagi's conviction for reset and in his deportation to Italy. It is surprising to note that the number of persons of Italian origin in and on the fringes of the underworld was fairly numerous, given that the Italian colony in Scotland at that time was only a fraction of what it is now.

There was also the legendary street bookie Laurie Ventre from the Garscube Road, of Italian parents, who over the years had acquired a Robin Hood-like reputation because of his generosity to the needy citizens of that neighbourhood. There was never a needy widow, or some other unfortunate who could not pay his rent or settle a debt, who did not benefit from Ventre's generosity. His death in the 1960s was mourned in the Garscube Road by a funeral to rival that of any Chicago Godfather, with carloads of flowers and hundreds of mourners who afterwards set new records for the amount of liquor consumed in the local pubs. The local constabulary was much in evidence too, not only to pay their respects to an esteemed and valued adversary, but also to keep the peace in the event of friction between the opposing factions present at the funeral.

Then there was Giuseppe Passarelli, who early in life became known as Gus Hart, the well known manager of Benny Lynch. Born into an Italian immigrant family, Passarelli rebelled at the strict Italian way of life of his parents and ran away from home at an early age to join the boxing booths in a circus. He was befriended by a family by the name of Hart, and he elected to be known by that name for the rest of his life. Despite his Italian background he escaped internment, and after the war he dabbled in a few enterprises in Glasgow. He met up with Benny Lynch, and towards the twilight of the boxer's career he took up the management of the ex-world champion. One night he and Benny Lynch were involved in a car crash, and although not badly injured, both were taken to hospital and kept in overnight for observation. On reading of the accident in a newspaper, Benny, who did not know Hart's real name, wanted to know where the third passenger by the name of Passarelli had come from!

A name that has gone down in infamy amongst the old generations of Italians is that of Dino Olivieri, a flag-waving member of the *Casa Del Fascio* who paraded his Italian patriotism ostentatiously before his fellow immigrants. Capitalising on the patriotic fervour engendered by the propaganda emanating from the palatial new building in Park Circus, he founded a bank, La Banca d'Italia, at the corner of Hope Street and Argyle Street. Every Italian family in the west of Scotland was canvassed and urged to deposit money in his new bank. Many of them did so, under the mistaken impression that La Banca d'Italia had the backing of the Italian government, and some, especially those dazzled by the image projected by the new Italy, deposited all of their hard-earned savings in Olivieri's bank. In 1938 the bank declared itself bankrupt, and the gullible depositors lost every single penny. Since there was a presumption of fraud, an investigation was mounted, but the affair was forgotten in the turmoil of the war. Forgotten, that is, except by those, and they were many, who lost the fruits of a lifetime of toil through the shady dealings of a man of doubtful honesty, who preyed on their misplaced and naïve love of their motherland. A justice of sorts was done, however. Olivieri was interned and went down on the *Arandora Star*. He did not drown, but sustained injuries which confined him to a wheelchair for the few remaining years of his life.

Without a doubt the most famous and honoured Italian immigrant to Scotland is Charles Forte of Trust House Forte fame. Lord Charles Forte was born in 1908 in the village of Monforte Casalaticco, in the province of Lazio. At the age of seven he and his mother joined his father in Alloa, where the elder Forte had established himself in the café business. The father was one of the ones who realised the importance of a proper education, and saw to it that his son was able to attend schools both in Alloa and later in Dumfries. Rather than go on to university, the boy elected to do practical and profitable work in the family café. At the age of 21 he took over the running of the business, and then in 1934 went to London where he opened the first of his famous milk bars. In common with all other Italians he was arrested on the outbreak of war with Italy, but was fortunate to find himself interned in a camp on the Isle of Man, where he was able to petition for an early release. After the war Forte expanded his business rapidly, and received numerous government catering contracts and the entire airline catering for Heathrow Airport. He even received the contract to cater for all of the food served at the 1951 Festival of Britain, an exhibition on the South Bank, London, which saw nearly 8½ million visitors in four months. Forte purchased his first hotel, the Waldorf in London, in 1958, and in 1962, his company was floated on the London Stock Exchange. His was the first company to recognize the importance of road travel, by opening the first motorway service area in Britain. In 1995 Forte PLC had become one of the largest hotel chains in the world, with 940 hotels, 400 restaurants and the Little Chef motor road caféteria chain, which between them employed tens of thousands of workers. Lord Forte received a knighthood in 1970, and was later elected to the peerage in 1982. He is a Knight of the Grand Cross of the Italian Republic, and was personally presented with a special Papal Medal by Pope Pious XII. Lord Forte is proud of his Italian roots and his Scottish background. Margaret Thatcher once said of him:

'Charles Forte is a man whose vision has never dimmed. When he founded his business he was equipped with two vital strengths, a clear sense of right and wrong inherited from his Italian parents and a sound education from his childhood in Scotland. By adding to these his own enterprise, determination and leadership, he has built a company which has provided billions of pounds in foreign earnings for our country and jobs for tens of thousands of people across the world.'

All of which is not at all bad for a young Italian immigrant who learned his trade behind the counter of his father's ice-cream shop.

Charles Forte's son Rocco was also knighted in 1995 for his services to tourism.

7

The War

The Second World War wreaked havoc amongst the Italian families in Scotland. As the months passed after Germany's invasion of Poland and the declaration of war by Britain against Germany, and as Mussolini gave no sign that he would enter the conflict on the side of his ally Hitler, an optimistic mood began to show itself in the Italian community. Perhaps Il Duce would remain neutral in this war, as Franco of Spain had declared himself to be, said the optimistic ones, and the Scottish Italians would be left to carry on as usual in their adopted land. Never a thought was given to what might result if the unthinkable were to happen. There was no time to think about it. War is always good for trade and money flowed freely. The cash registers of the ice-cream and chip shops had never been so active, and any worries the immigrants may have harboured as to what might happen if Italy were to go to war on the side of the Germans had been pushed to the back of their minds.

Suddenly, on the afternoon of 10 June 1940, all euphoria vanished. France had all but fallen to the German Blitzkrieg, the British Army was in retreat at Dunkirk, and Mussolini, in an act which was described by many as a stab in the back of a dying man, declared war on Britain. The effect on the Italian community was devastating. On that day the 4,000 or so Italians in Scotland suddenly became enemy aliens, and as such posed a problem for the government. Although about 3,000 of these were women and children and were no conceivable threat to Britain, a good percentage of the remaining male members of the Italian community were of military age and could possibly have constituted a dangerous fifth column in the event of an Axis invasion of Britain, an invasion which now seemed to be imminent and certain. Moreover, a good proportion of these Italians were members of the Casa del Fascio, and therefore members of the Fascist party.

The words 'Fifth Column' had a pertinent and sinister meaning in those days. They had their origin in the recently finished Spanish Civil War, at the time when Franco began his advance on Madrid in July 1936 with four columns of rebel soldiers. As he advanced on the capital without meeting any organised resistance on the part of the government forces, the garrison of the Alcazar in Toledo south of Madrid, which had come out on the side of Franco, was put under siege by soldiers still loyal to the legally constituted government. Franco was advised by his generals not to divert to Toledo to lift the siege on his allies, since a delay of the month or more necessary for the lifting of the siege would enable Madrid to organise its defences. This advice was rejected by him with the remark that he had a fifth column of hidden rebels in the capital which would rise at the appropriate time and help conquer the city from within. This so-called 'Fifth Column' was simply a fiction invented by Franco to weaken the morale of the Government forces and never existed, but the phrase was taken up internationally, and frequently used in Britain to describe any fascist and Nazi sympathisers who might rise up and give help to invaders.

On the day of Italy's declaration of war, the question of what should be done about the Italians in the country came up during an emergency meeting of the British War Cabinet, and the problem of separating the obviously harmless from the potentially dangerous was discussed. At the end of the meeting Churchill cut across all argument and is reported to have issued the following short, sharp order: 'Collar the lot!'

An order went out to all police stations in Great Britain that all male Italians between the age of 16 and 70 should be arrested immediately and interned. This order was carried out by the police to the letter and beyond. When the arrests were begun, many old men of nearly 80 were caught up in the net, as were some boys as young as 14. The Italians of Scotland were never able to understand why the arrests should have been so indiscriminate. There is no doubt whatsoever that there were some fascists and Axis sympathisers among the male Italian population who could have constituted a danger in the event of an Axis invasion of Britain, and these should have been interned. Britain, however, had already been at war for nine months with Germany, and all the signs were that Italy was standing by her ally. It should have been possible in that time for the British government to have singled out the potentially dangerous elements from the great mass of mainly harmless Italians. Even though this obviously had not been done, the identities of those who might have constituted a danger to Britain could quickly have been established by a glance at the membership lists of the Casa Del Fascio, which must have become available to the police when the premises were taken over immediately at the outbreak of war. Moreover, every alien over 16 years of age, male or female, had by law to carry an aliens identity book, where every movement of the person concerned was duly recorded by the police. In addition, the Italians in Scotland were almost all café and chip shop owners, and well known to the local police. It should have been patently obvious to the police authorities that the vast majority of registered Italian aliens constituted no threat of any kind to anybody, no matter what the circumstances.

Despite all this, almost all male Italians in the age group mentioned found themselves in prison cells just a few hours after Mussolini's declaration of war. The injustice of some of these arrests was beyond belief. Men who had fought in the British Army during the First World War were arrested. Fathers with sons on active service in the British Army found themselves in prison cells. Men who had dedicated their lives to fighting fascism, and who could never have returned to Italy because of their political views, found themselves behind bars. The son of one of these internees, Sergeant Santangeli of Pollokshaws, who had just returned from the battles in France and the evacuation of Dunkirk, and who had come home to find the family café in Pollokshaws Road wrecked and boarded up and his father nowhere to be found, spent days looking for his parent. He was finally given the information that the old man had been arrested, and he went berserk with rage at the sight of his 75-year-old father standing forlornly behind a barbed wire fence in a prison camp in Woodhouselea.

Giacomo Martorana, a young 20-year-old Italian-American on a visit to relations in Glasgow, and who had received his calling up papers from the American army some days before, was arrested and together with 403 others was shipped off to a POW camp in Canada. After six months of imprisonment, during which he constantly bombarded the authorities with complaints about the illegality of his arrest, he was finally able to convince them that his imprisonment had been a mistake. He was released to join the American Army. He died in June 1943 on Omaha Beach on D-Day, where he earned a Purple Heart medal for his bravery in taking out a German machine-gun fortification. Silvestro D'Ambrosio was a 68-year-old from Hamilton who had lived in Scotland for 42 years. His application for British citizenship had been pending since the outbreak of war. Two of his sons were serving in the British Army and another in the Canadian Army, and yet on 10 June he was arrested and lost his life a month or so later in the sinking of the *Arandora Star*. Arturo Filippi was a Scots-Italian from Ayr serving in the British Army. His feelings can be imagined when he found himself standing guard over his interned father, who stood staring at him from behind the wire at Woodhouselea camp in Midlothian. Alberto Loria, an Italian Jew, had come to Britain in 1911, had a British wife, two British-born daughters and had been awarded an OBE for his work with the British Ministry of Munitions. He was arrested the day after the outbreak of war. Decio Anzani was the secretary of the Italian section of the League of the Rights of Man in London, an organisation whose anti-fascist activities were well known throughout Europe. He had lived in this country for 31 years, unable to return to Italy because of his political views, and was one of the best known anti-fascists in Britain. He was on a visit to Glasgow on 10 June on the invitation of the Scottish branch of the Labour Party to address a meeting there, and was arrested that same night. He too lost his life in the sinking of the *Arandora Star*.

Within recent years, an Italian journalist, Arturo Bernabei, has written a series of articles in the national newspaper *L'Unita* which examine the internment of Italian civilians in June 1940, and comments on the curious fact that many well known and politically active anti-fascist Italians resident here were arrested immediately on the outbreak of war. Russia had as yet not been invaded by the Nazis, and was not as yet an ally of Britain; indeed, the Berlin-Warsaw non-aggression pact which had been followed by the invasion of Poland and the division of that country between Hitler and Stalin was still very much in British politicians' minds. Bernabei maintains that as far as the government of Winston Churchill was concerned, Russia and international communism were basically as big a threat in the long term as was Hitler, and were a threat that would eventually have to be dealt with.

For this reason, Italian anti-fascists and exiles abroad, who were all extremely left-wing, were probably much more dangerous to Britain in the long run than Mussolini and the fascists were. Moreover, these groups, and in particular Decio Anzani, were known to have contact with Togliatti, the communist party leader who had fled Italy with the coming of fascism and who now lived in exile in Moscow. The British government's priority, according to Bernabei, was the maintenance 'of the moderating influence of the Church and the Monarchy' in Italy. Since the policy of the left wing exiles would have done away with both these institutions after the eventual defeat of fascism, leaving the country open to communist dominance, then these exiles and anti-fascists should be treated as being in every way as dangerous to British interests as were the fascists they opposed. Bernabei claims that it was for this reason that an offer on the part of Italian political exiles 'to form an anti-Mussolini Italian government abroad' made by Decio Anzani in the early part of 1939, was refused. In any event, the problem was solved for the British government by Gunther Prien when he fired his torpedo and

A group of chestnut harvesters in Bacchionero in the early 1900s

Soldiers in the Italian army in 1917. In the centre is author's father, Francesco Pieri

Italian street vendor

*Some Scots-Italians progressed from street-vending to ownership of their own premises.
This is Albert Risi's father at his London Road cafe, 1906*

(Left) The author with his father, mother and older brother, Glasgow 1922. (Right) Marcello Di Tano as a boy, with mother and grandmother, 1930

A grandparent now himself, Marcello Di Tano with his granddaughters Annalisa and Francesca

The author's Alien's Registration pass book

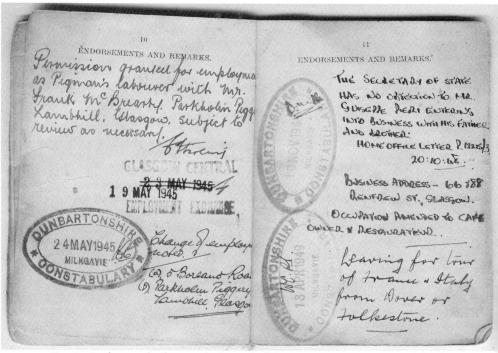

Entries in the pass book towards the end of the war—permission granted for the author's employment as a pigman's labourer!

Rando Bertoia, only living survivor of the sinking of the Arandora Star, *in Glasgow*

Wire around the internment camp on Ile St Helene, Montreal

Italians and Scots-Italians in the Bar Capretz, Barga, during the 1930s. Among the group are Sandrino and Enrico Nardini (courtesy of Ale Nardini)

Wedding in Glasgow between the Pelosi and D'Artino families

Italian dance at St Thomas' Church Hall, Glasgow

A gathering of the Scots-Italian Golfing Society

The leading businessman Dave Coia, with his portrait by Emilio Coia

The author with his late wife, Mary

sank the *Arandora Star*, for almost every single one of the anti-fascist Italians living in Britain died with it. The historian Gaetano Salvemini takes the same line, and goes further to claim that the sending of the *Arandora Star* into submarine-infested waters, armed with cannons and with no red cross markings and loaded as she was with civilians penned in behind barbed wire, could well be labelled as a war crime.

The list of the unjustly interned could go on and on and on. To be fair, it has to be said that there were many Labour members of Parliament who questioned the manner of the internment of Italians. Many Labour politicians, in particular Herbert Morrison, who later was to become Home Secretary in Churchill's coalition government, had actively sponsored Decio Anzani and his colleagues and were asking embarrassing questions in Parliament about their internment. Under pressure from them, the Home Secretary of the day, Sir John Anderson, was forced to state that the arrest of many of the Italians was not 'a preconsidered political measure against Italian elements of the left who were looked upon with suspicion because of their sympathy with the Soviet Union', and that the internment of Decio Anzani and his colleagues was due to 'an administrative error'. He went on to declare:

> 'I am not here to deny for a moment that the most regrettable and the most deplorable things have happened... they have been partly due to the haste with which the policy of internment had to be carried out. They have been due in some cases to the mistakes of individuals and to stupidity and muddle. These matters all relate to the past. So far as we can remedy mistakes we shall remedy them.'

In the summer of 1941 Herbert Morrison had taken the place of Sir John Anderson as Home Secretary, and one of his first tasks was to review the whole question of the internment of Aliens. As a result of this, Home Office representatives were sent to the various camps on the Isle of Man and to Camp 43 in Montreal to interview prisoners and offer some of them repatriation to Britain. Mr Patterson, the Home Office official who was sent to Camp 43 in Montreal, and who remained there for three months to interview prisoners, was startled to find that not only were there very few fascist sympathisers to be found in the camp amongst the civilians there, but also that a substantial number of the Italian prisoners had been born in the UK and could not speak a single word of Italian! As a result of his visit about 50 of the internees were taken back to Britain and released. It does not need to be said of course that repatriation to the UK could not be offered to the 446 Italians who had perished on the *Arandora Star*.

An example which encapsulates the indiscriminate nature of the application of government policy in the matter of the internment of Italians is that of Giuseppe Martinez, an Italian national who had set up and was at that time general manager of the Pirelli factory in Southampton. At the beginning of the war with Germany in 1939, the British merchant fleet had begun to suffer very heavy losses because of the Germans' use of a new naval weapon, the magnetic mine. These sea mines were placed at undetectable depths in the busy sea-lanes around the British coast and were detonated by the proximity of a magnetic field such as that generated by the mass of iron in the hull of a ship. This new weapon caused consternation at the Admiralty, for the losses sustained by Allied shipping would soon have paralyzed Britain's only supply line.

To counter this threat and to render the magnetic mines ineffective, the Pirelli boffins, under the direct supervision of Giuseppe Martinez, came up with a solution: the degaussing cable. This consisted of a thick wire cable to be fitted under and around the hull of a ship. An electric current of determined strength was then passed through the cable, thus producing an electrical field which neutralised the magnetic field created by the metallic mass of the vessel. As a result, the magnetic mines hidden below the surface of the sea were rendered ineffective. Within the matter of a few weeks, all Allied shipping was equipped with degaussing cables, many of which were produced under the supervision of Giuseppe Martinez at his Southampton factory. Despite this most important contribution to the war effort, within a matter of hours of Italy's declaration of war, and without interrogation or investigation, Giuseppe Martinez was arrested with his eldest son Carlo. After a stay at the dreadful Warth Mills camp they found themselves together with several hundred other Italians on a dock at Liverpool slowly being loaded on to the *Arandora Star*. There the only space they could find to lie down was a section of the upper deck which fortunately was not covered in with barbed wire. From there they were blasted into the open sea by the impact of Gunther Prien's torpedo. For several hours they floated on the debris-covered sea, surrounded by the dead and dying, until rescued by a Canadian destroyer and taken to the Clyde port of Greenock. On 9 July, together with hundreds of other survivors from the *Arandora Star*, they were taken by train to Liverpool and marched onto another converted cruise ship, the *Dunera,* which docked two months later in Australia. The atrocious conditions aboard that ship have been well documented.

As an added shock to the trauma of the arrests of their menfolk, Italian families in Scotland were subjected to a further ordeal on the night of Mussolini's declaration of war. That night gangs of hooligans took to the streets of Scottish towns and cities to vent their rage on Italians and their property. On 10 June there was hardly a café or fish and chip shop in the land which was not wrecked, broken into, looted and vandalised. In the book *Isle of the Displaced* I describe the scene as our own shop was looted. At the time I lived in a flat directly above the shop premises.

'A muted roar made itself heard from the street below, rising to a crescendo of shouting voices directly under my window. I went over and peered out through the curtains. A crowd of about a hundred shouting and gesticulating people, pushing in front of them a handcart loaded with stones and bricks, were gathering in front of the shop. 'There's a Tally place... do it in!', came the shout; then to an accompaniment of yells and cheers, a barrage of missiles came flying through the air, smashing into the glass frontage of the shop. A dozen or so of the mob, armed with sticks and batons, cleared away the jagged edges of the broken windows and jumped through into the shop beyond. Through a curiously detached and dreamlike mental haze I could hear the sound of smashing and curses from below, and peering fearfully through the lace curtains, I watched as the contents of the looted shop were distributed to the milling crowd. That night there were few, if any, Italian shops left untouched by the gangs of hooligans, and although no physical harm was done to anyone, years of hard work was destroyed by unrestrained bands of louts who roamed the streets of Glasgow wrecking and looting in the name of patriotism. As far as I know, not a finger was lifted by the police in an attempt to stop the looting of Italian shops in Glasgow that night.'

The next day the London *Times* carried reports of anti-Italian riots in Soho, Liverpool, Edinburgh and Glasgow, and reported that Edinburgh was the worst affected.

'The most riotous scenes occurred in Leith Street and Union Place, where a crowd of over a thousand had gathered, many of them in the role of spectators. Several persons were injured, and

numerous arrests were made during these anti-Italian demon-
strations and police had to make baton charges to check and
disperse the angry crowds.'

The Edinburgh *Evening News* reported on 12 June:

'Leith Street and Leith Walk looked in places as if a series of
heavy bombs had fallen. In Italian premises not a scrap of glass
remained in any window, furniture broken, window frames
destroyed and contents of the shops looted. Shop premises in
Antigua Street and Broughton Street were set on fire. More
than a score of the rioters were treated in Leith Hospital for
injuries and cuts caused by broken glass.'

The looting and burning of Italian shops was more widespread and particularly vicious in Scotland, probably because of the added ingredient of the
religious bigotry prevalent there. Italians were obviously Catholic, and one
has only to examine the pre-war history of rabid sectarianism in Edinburgh
and to a lesser extent in Glasgow to understand the reaction of a certain
section of the public to Mussolini's declaration of war. In Edinburgh during
the 1930s, the Protestant Action party under the leadership of the dema-
gogue John Cormack had campaigned openly against Catholicism, and as he
put it, 'the menace of Rome and of Irish immigration'. His party won 31
percent of the vote in the local council elections of 1938, this only a few
months after his anti-Catholic oratory had incited a riot in front of St Andrew's
Church in Canaan Lane. In those days the uninformed masses could be moved
by fanatical oratory to carry out deeds they would ordinarily never contem-
plate. On looking back over the destruction of Italian shops on the night of
Mussolini's declaration of war, however, it has to be remembered that the
vast majority of Scots took no part in and actively deplored the actions of a
few on that night of 10 June 1940.

There then followed another incredible and tragic decision on the part of
the Government. After some weeks of captivity about 1000 or so of these
Italian internees, some from Scotland, some from England, were picked out,
nobody has ever explained on what basis, and sent to a camp at Warth Mills
near Liverpool. The journey of the Scottish-Italians selected started at the
Garrioch Road railway station in Glasgow, and the prisoners were marched
there from Maryhill barracks, where they had been kept after a stay in the
police cells. The following is another quotation from *Isle of the Displaced*.

'On the morning of the fourth day at the barracks, after the usual breakfast of strong tea, bread, margarine and jam, we were told to get all our belongings together, and after a short wait in the compound, we were marched out under heavy guard into the street. Word of the imminent appearance of the prisoners had spread and the pavements of Maryhill Road were lined with hundreds of curiosity-seekers straining to get a view of the marching men. I tried to keep in some sort of step with my companions and tried to keep my head held high. I'm not going to show any fear or despondency to these people, I thought, with the events of that first night, the arrest, the smashing of our shop, still vivid in my mind. But the crowds lining the streets were strangely muted, in sharp contrast to the mobs which had taken to the streets on the night of the arrests, and although a few jeers were shouted at the prisoners, very few voices could be heard above the sound of scuffling feet. We must have presented a curious sight to the onlookers. Ranging from 16-year-old youths to bent old men in their seventies, unshaven and unwashed and wearing clothes which had been slept in for more than a week, we did not seem to constitute much of a threat to anyone. Our destination was a railway siding in Garrioch Road, some 500 yards from the barracks gates in Maryhill Road, and with the short walk soon completed, we were made to assemble on the station platform to await the next leg of our journey.

The day was hot and sunny as we sat and waited, and the warm weather seemed to engender a mood of euphoria in us. We chattered and joked and the guards, some of whom were known to us as customers in our shops, relaxed with us, exchanging non-committal remarks and offering us the occasional cigarette. On the station platform there was a ticket office manned by a solitary elderly railway employee, who stood watching the proceedings with curiosity. He paused for a while, then came out to the platform, took a packet of Capstan from his pocket, and offered some cigarettes to the waiting prisoners with the words, "Good luck to you wherever you're going. We're all Jock Tamson's bairns".

I cannot say whether the thanks directed to him were for the cigarettes or for the words of comfort, but the prisoners were profuse in their thanks and acknowledgement.'

The prisoners' destination was Wharf Mills, a derelict cotton mill in Bury. It was an old building, a disintegrating relic of the Industrial Revolution which had lain disused since the end of the First World War and was now falling to pieces. It was rat-infested, with broken windows and gaping holes in the roof. Stripped of its machinery, the stone floor was greasy and oily with disintegrating cotton rags everywhere. A fine dust hung in the air. There was no electricity: the only illumination was the daylight which filtered through the dirty cracked windows and broken glass panels which formed part of the roof. Into this Dickensian scene were packed about 3,000 persons, German and Italian civilians and Jewish refugees. The stench was well nigh unbearable. The original lavatory facilities, blackened and stained by long years of disuse, were totally inadequate and had been augmented by latrines dug into the ground outside the mill. There were a few cold-water taps to meet the needs of thousands of prisoners, and the simple act of washing one's hands required long periods of queuing. A double fence of barbed wire about seven feet high, constantly patrolled by armed guards, had been erected around the perimeter and hundreds of men stood, sat or squatted as near to it as possible, preferring the open air to the squalor of the interior. At least the camp at Woodhouselea had provided a clean environment with plenty of fresh air, but at Warth Mills it was as though the portals of Dante's Inferno had opened up. The sights, sounds and smells of the place were dreadful.

This is part of the International Red Cross report on the camp:

> 'Cotton waste littered the entrance and the floor was slippery with oil and grease. The mill was lit only through the glass roof; as many of its panes were broken or missing, it also let in the rain which collected in large puddles below. There were eighteen cold water taps for each 500 men and the lavatories were filthy... the food was sparse: the evening meal consisted of a lump of bread, a small piece of cheese and a cup of tea. There were few mattresses at first and most internees slept on boards covered by two or three blankets, some of which proved verminous. At night they could hear rats scuttling among the remnants of the mill machinery. The entire building was surrounded by two fences of barbed wire, with armed guards patrolling in between.'

The Red Cross, which was performing its traditional neutral role of trying to secure adequate conditions for prisoners of war, singled out the absence of lighting, the poor hygiene, which included the small number of taps, the absence of hot water and the lack of lavatories. The Geneva-based International Committee of the Red Cross, through its delegate in Britain, also criticized the camp's inadequate sick-bay, with only thirty beds for the 250 internees who were ill and required treatment.

Fortunately Wharf Mills served only as a transit camp and had to be endured for no more than a week or ten days. One morning 400 Italian names were read out and their owners loaded onto a train bound for the Liverpool docks. This was the scene at the dockside:

'We had not eaten since we had left Warth Mills that morning, and the pangs of hunger and thirst added to our general misery. Some time after the departure of the ship named *Arandora Star*, another ship drew into the side of the quay. This ship bore the name *Ettrick* and seemed to be somewhat smaller than the one that had just sailed, but it too was painted a dull grey, had coils of wire visible on the deck, and had a large gun mounted at the stern. Again a gangway was run up to the deck, and orders to move up were issued. An army lorry was stationed at the entrance to the gangway, and as we shuffled past each of us was thrown a paper bag, which was full of hard-tack biscuits. The group from Warth Mills had remained intact, and as I moved up the gangway I looked behind to see that the German POWs were following on behind us. The deck area at the top of the gangplank was completely sealed off with barbed wire, and behind this stood members of the ship's crew watching the proceedings with curiosity. We had little time to examine our surroundings, for no sooner had we taken a few steps along the deck, than we were made to descend into the bowels of the ship, urged on by a choleric little sergeant who stood at the top of a flight of stairs shouting abuse as we passed by. The accommodation in which we found ourselves was small and cramped, and consisted of four large hold-like areas connected by a narrow passage. The space was completely devoid of furnishings and afforded barely enough space for everyone to lie down at the same time. A row of portholes on one side was sealed up and the sole illumination consisted of a few bulkhead lights high on the ceiling. Ventilation was through gratings on the wall and although the place seemed clean enough, the space available was totally inadequate for the 400 men crammed in there. As one of the first into the area I immediately found myself a place on the floor with my back to the wall near the entrance and there I sat patiently to await developments.

At 6am the next morning the *Ettrick* set sail. As soon as she left the dock the guards were withdrawn and a group of us hurried out on deck. The implication of what we saw there did not immediately sink in. A section of the deck about 20 feet long and a few feet wide had been caged off with barbed wire which stretched from the deck to the roof above it, and sealed off the area completely. This left a passage to the section of the ship which housed the German POWs, some of whom were already breathing in the fresh air on deck. A barbed wire gate to the open deck was heavily padlocked and guarded on the outside by two armed soldiers, while from the other side of the wire a handful of crew members stared curiously at the caged prisoners. The two groups of prisoners, Italian internees in one hold and the German POWs in the other, nearly a thousand men all told, were effectively sealed off from the rest of the ship, with a heavily padlocked wire gate as the only point of exit in the event of an emergency. To the prisoners on the *Ettrick* the peril of our situation was only too apparent. Imprisoned as we were in the hold behind the fences of barbed wire, in the event of an emergency we would be caught like rats in a trap and would perish without the slightest hope of escape.'

❀ 8 ❀

Anomalies

Some Scottish-Italians found themselves in somewhat unusual situations at the outbreak of war with Italy—some of them not without an element of humour.

In Glasgow, the son of the owner of the Strand Café in Dumbarton Road at the entrance to Partick underground station was a certain Sam Forte, who from an early age had helped his father to run the café. Sam's parents had emigrated to Scotland from the Naples area in the early 1900s and although Sam himself was born in Glasgow, he had inherited strong emotional attachments to the country of his parent's birth. When still an impressionable boy in the late 1920s, he would listen to his father extolling the virtues of Il Duce, whom he saw as the saviour of Italy from the dark forces of Bolshevism. The young Sam was encourage by his father to frequent the newly formed Casa Del Fascio, and there he learned of the *Balilla*, an organisation for boys and youths modelled on the Boy Scout movement in Britain, but with a distinct difference. The *Balilla* was purely military in concept: the boys wore smart black uniforms with a tasselled cap, trained with imitation guns and underwent a disciplined regime, all this in holiday camps set in some of the most beautiful parts of Italy.

Apart from the quasi-military training, all kinds of sporting events and social activities were laid on for the boys, and Sam was encouraged to take part in this new movement. In the exciting environment of the *Balilla* camps, young Sam found escape from the daily monotony of his work in the family café and moreover, the *Balilla* paid all travel expenses for its recruits, so the visits to Italy were in effect free holidays for the boy. Then in 1936, civil war erupted in Spain, a war in which communist Russia sided with the republican government of Spain, with Germany and Italy supporting the right-wing Franco rebels. This support soon took the form of material intervention in the war. Russia sent tanks, artillery, munitions and military advisers to the Republican side, Germany sent part of her Luftwaffe, the Condor Legion, to assist Franco, whilst Mussolini, not to be outdone, decided to send two full divisions of volunteers to fight side by side with Franco's troops. The young Sam was caught up in the storm of propaganda which had swept through Italy. Here was the Bolshevik enemy trying to establish a foothold in the Mediterranean; here was the opportunity for the glorious youth of Italy to fight against the Communist enemy, etc, etc, blared the radio and press. Sam, now about 18 years of age, was caught up in the national hysteria, and in a burst of patriotic fervour, found himself as a volunteer in the Italian divisions sent to fight in Spain.

Some time later, pinned down by enemy fire on the hills of Guadalajara, some 30 miles from Madrid, he came face to face with the reality of war, an experience far removed from the glamorous atmosphere of the *Balilla* camps. Here men were being killed in a variety of ghastly ways, bodies ripped open by bullets, limbs torn off by explosions, human beings with their brains and guts spilled open and freezing in the icy mud and sleet of a Spanish winter. with not a hint of the glamour and glory he had been conditioned to expect from the years of visits to the *Balilla* camps. Sam was not a cowardly man, however, and during an action which resulted in his unit becoming isolated he stayed behind to help his Captain, who had been badly wounded in the legs. He dragged him under fire to the comparative safety of a ruined farmhouse building, and during the cover of night Sam carried the unconscious man on his back to their own unit, now regrouped some miles back.

The fascist propaganda machine back in Rome had been churning out all sorts of fictitious accounts about imaginary victories against the Bolshevik armies in Spain, and here finally was a true event, a courageous action carried out by an ex-*Balilla* recruit, which could be used as a morale-building story to maintain enthusiasm among the public for the Duce's intervention in the Spanish conflict. Sam was commended by his Colonel and returned as a conquering hero to Rome, where he was summoned by the great Duce himself to be presented with a military decoration for his bravery in saving the life of his commanding officer. Being only human, Sam revelled in the adulation showered upon him, but his pleasure in all these events was tempered by the arrival of a letter from his father in Glasgow. His parent was not well, his mother too was ailing, and his presence was required back home to help carry on the family shop. So after a few months, his exploit now forgotten by the press, he was granted unlimited compassionate leave by the Army, to find himself once more behind the Strand café counter in Glasgow, with his desire for further adventure extinguished by the reality of his war experience in Spain.

Strangely enough, yet perhaps not so strangely, for in those days news reportage of an international nature was by no means comprehensive, not a single word of his exploits had percolated back to Glasgow. As a British subject born in Britain, Sam was free to come and go as he pleased without check or hindrance by the British authorities. As far as his acquaintances and customers were concerned, Sam had just been away for a couple of years for no apparent reason. Moreover at that time, because of the worsening international situation and with Mussolini sliding into his military pacts with Hitler, Sam thought it prudent to keep the story of his military adventures in the Italian army strictly to himself.

Then in 1940 Italy declared war on Britain, and on that very day Sam, as the British subject that he was, received calling up papers from the British Army, and was ordered to report to Maryhill barracks to begin his military service. Sam had no desire whatsoever to serve in any army, his experiences on the cold Guadalajara plateau had cured him of any desire to play soldier, plus the fact that he did not relish the possibility of fighting against the very comrades he had served with not so long ago. He thought long and hard about his situation, and was still thinking as he stood to attention in front of a recruitment officer in a room at the barracks. He waited as the officer consulted some papers.

'Now Forte, I see here that your parents were born in Italy?'

'Yes, sir,' answered Sam, with a little nervous cough.

'Do you speak Italian?' Conveniently forgetting that he was equally at home in both languages Sam pondered for a second.

'A wee bit, sir.'

'You know that Italy is now at war with us, so I'll have to get some background before I find a post for you. Can you drive a car? Were you ever in the Boy Scouts? Were you ever in the Cubs? Have you any special ability?

Sam coughed again. 'No Sir, I've never been in the Scouts, but I served for nearly two years in the Littorio division of the Italian Army under General Roatta, and fought in the battle of Guadalajara in Spain,' again a little cough. 'And I was decorated by Mussolini with the Silver Military Cross for bravery in action.'

He spread out his Italian military papers in front of the speechless Major, topped them off with a glossy photograph of a beaming Duce in the act of pinning a decoration on his chest, gave another little cough, then leaned back to await reactions.

A flabbergasted Major pawed feverishly through the papers, and stopped to stare for several seconds at the photo of Sam standing stiffly to attention in front of his Duce. His face changed through several different colours, finally settling into a vivid puce. He let out a roar and had Sam taken immediately to be locked up in the detention cells.

And there Sam languished for nearly a week. A battery of Intelligence Officers questioned him intensively about his *Balilla* activities and his military service in Spain. Through it all he felt quite badly done to. What had he done after all? Britain wasn't at war with Italy during his period of military service, so what was everyone on about? The questions exhausted, Sam was interned under wartime regulation 18B, a law that allowed of the imprisonment of any person, irrespective of country of origin, who was deemed to be of danger to the State. Thus he remained for the best part of six months until released as a volunteer to serve in the Home Pioneer Corps, a branch of the Army whose work it was to clear the rubble from the bombed cities of Britain. That, reasoned Sam, was better than vegetating behind barbed wire for the duration of the war, to be faced afterwards with a very uncertain future. After all, the family café would probably be there to go back to after the end of the war and his customers would not be able to point the finger of scorn at him for not having served his country of birth well during the conflict.

The war ended and Sam returned to his post behind the counter of the Strand Café, which, in common with many other cafés in Glasgow, had been smashed up on the first night of the war. On one of the walls of the shop there hangs a photo of himself as a sergeant in the British Army, the rank attained during his service in the Pioneer Corps. Prominently displayed in the privacy of his home there is a framed photographic enlargement of his day of glory in Rome.

Together with his brother Joe, Freddie Guidi was the owner of two well known Glasgow restaurants. Both were situated at the Hope Street end of Argyle Street, near the Alhambra Theatre. One, the Alhambra Restaurant, was a busy fish and chip shop, and the other, the Copra, just a few yards away, was a full restaurant with a well varied menu. The way they ran the business made it possible for the two brothers to take extensive holidays, which Freddie usually spent in the town of his parents' birth, Barga, in the province of Lucca. He was there at the outbreak of war with Germany in 1939, and was flabbergasted to receive calling-up papers from the Italian army. He was not aware that the Italian government considered all persons born of Italian parents as Italian subjects, no matter where they themselves had been born, so he found himself training in a barracks in Libya when Italy declared war on Britain in June 1940. As a still raw recruit he saw action in the various see-saw battles with British troops in the Libyan desert, and his military career as an Italian soldier came to an abrupt end on his capture by newly landed American troops in an action on the Tunisian border. Being completely bilingual he was put to work as an interpreter by his captors, and since his own uniform was by now in tatters, he was issued with American fatigue clothing to wear, making him to all intents and purposes an American soldier. After six months or so it came to the attention of his captors that their prisoner was British-born, and so he was handed over to the British authorities. He was able to convince the British military that he had been literally dragooned into the Italian Army and that he was anything but a fascist sympathiser, and so he was given a British uniform and assigned to a Scottish regiment for service.

He trained with his new companions for several months, then found himself being shot at on a Normandy beach by the Germans on the occasion of the Allied invasion of France on D-Day. Once the German defences had been breached, his regiment fanned out into the surrounding countryside, where, after some days of sporadic action, he was taken prisoner by a German patrol. After weeks of travel and travail he reached his final destination, a German POW camp in Cracow, Poland. There he spent the rest of the war until his liberation by the advancing Russians. One year later he was back at the counter of the Alhambra restaurant, serving fish suppers to the Glasgow public, who were blissfully unaware that the Tally behind the counter had served in each of the two opposing armies in the recently finished war.

Toni was born in Scotland of Italian parents and English was his native tongue. He had taken his soft Scottish accent with him to Italy when his parents took him back there to live at the age of 14 in 1934. Already bilingual, for only Italian had been spoken at home in Scotland, he continued his schooling in Italy, and graduated as a teacher of English from a college in the northern Italian town of Udine in 1940, just in time to be conscripted into the Italian army on the occasion of Mussolini's declaration of war on Britain. Because of his University degree he was given the rank of Lieutenant and posted to a counter-intelligence unit in Rome, where he had to translate documents from Italian to English and vice versa. The war began to go badly for Italy. Defeats were suffered in North Africa, the Germans sent the Afrika Korps to fight there and Toni was posted to the Folgore division stationed at Tobruk, where he was given the job of interrogating British soldiers captured in the various desert skirmishes. The Italian high command had desperate need of intelligence regarding British troop movements and dispositions. The RAF had complete command of the air, and any observation planes the Italians sent over enemy lines were guaranteed never to return to base, The Italian divisions and the Afrika Korps were literally fighting blind, with very little knowledge of what was happening behind the daily patrol skirmishes in the desert.

One day Toni was ordered to report to military headquarters at Tobruk. His fluency in English had been noted and he was asked to confirm that his speech was indistinguishable from that of a Scotsman. He was then asked to volunteer for a very dangerous task. The Axis armies were completely in the dark about British troop dispositions, and they desperately needed eye-witness observations done on the ground. Would he be willing to put on a British uniform, to be dropped off somewhere behind enemy lines, make any observations he could, then be picked up after a few days with whatever intelligence he had been able to gather? The idea was not as crazy as it sounded. Battles in the desert were sometimes chaotic and very fluid. Most encounters took place between highly mobile armoured groups, and it was no uncommon thing for individual soldiers to be separated from their unit and wander round the desert in search of their unit. If he were given the proper uniform and authentic papers, could Toni pull off a deception? Could he pretend to be a British soldier, a junior officer, say, in search of his unit? Could he wander around and pick up all the information he could then rejoin the Italian lines? He had to realise the danger. If his deception were uncovered he would be shot out of hand as a spy. Toni thought long and hard about it. His English, with its slight touch of Scottish accent, was idiomatically faultless. His appearance, given his northern Italian ancestry, was more Nordic than Latin, and he had absolutely no doubt that he could pass muster on these two counts. But would he have the nerve to sustain such a deception in what were bound to be nerve-wracking circumstances?

About two weeks later, Toni was sitting in a small caterpillar-wheeled troop-carrier, kitted out in the uniform of a British lieutenant. Round his neck was an identity disc bearing the name 'Thomas Martin', and in his tunic pocket were documents identifying him as belonging to the 13th Corps of the 8th Indian Division of the British Army. Driving along behind the troop carrier was a battered jeep, the very one the lieutenant had been in with two companions at the time of his capture. They moved on through the pitch-dark night, south to Wadi El Taqa and into the Quattara depression. There Toni carried on alone in the jeep, having made arrangements to be met there in exactly 24 hours. He carried on east, until he reckoned on being behind enemy lines, then swung north towards Wadi el Regel and the El Alamein area. Dawn broke. After a few more miles he sighted a group of armoured vehicles on the horizon, and approached slowly, yelling in English and waving as hard as he could. The vehicles were manned by French troops; their officer spoke English, so Toni told his story: lost on patrol, his companion killed, and he was trying to rejoin the 13th Corps. The French officer directed him to go further on, and Toni did so, passing behind row upon row of heavy artillery standing silent beside heaps of shells, with hundreds of tanks deployed at intervals. He had seen enough. An attack was obviously in preparation and he turned back towards the Quattara depression to his rendezvous point. As he neared his pick-up point the bombardment started. He had never seen or heard such a sight: the northern sky was bright with the muzzle flashes of big guns, and the attendant swell of noise made it sound as though all the thunder in Africa had been unleashed above him. He had read in his history books about the massed artillery bombardments on the Western front during the First World War, and he thought to himself that this is what it must have been like.

The guns went on without interruption for hours, then as dawn broke there was a sudden silence. The pick-up party had not appeared, and as he drove on a terrible sight awaited him. The ground was strewn with dead bodies and burnt out armour and lorries. Smoke and the stench of burnt cordite hung over everything and not living soul was to be seen. The ground was criss-crossed with the tracks of many vehicles and cries of pain could be heard from amongst the wreckage. Some soldiers in British uniform lay among the heaps of dead. Toni thought furiously. God alone only knew where his unit was, if now it existed at all. No sound of gunfire was to be heard in the still and silent air; he knew how fast advances and retreats could be in the desert; his comrades, if alive, could be scores of miles away. If he were found there in a British uniform he was as good as dead, for he would be executed as a spy. He started to search, and found a dead Italian of more or less his own size. Half the man's head had been torn away by shrapnel, but apart from some bloodstains his uniform was untouched. Toni stripped off his British uniform and put on the dead Italian's, together with his identity tags. He drove off half a mile or so into the desert and buried his British uniform beside the dead soldier.

His name was now Andrea Rotella, and he came from Cassino. Back amongst the ruined vehicles and dead bodies, he cut his head deeply with a piece of shrapnel until blood flowed, then hit his head against the side of a ruined tank until he lay in a pool of his own blood, and was eventually picked up by British burial patrols to be taken to a dressing station, then on to a transit camp in Egypt, then on to a British POW camp at the Gairloch in

Scotland. On his return to Italy at the end of the war, such was the post-war chaos there that he was able to revert to his true identity, and in 1949 was able to return to Scotland to join with a Glasgow Italian girl he had met whilst on working parties from the Gairloch camp. He married and prospered in business in Tillicoultry, where he died some years ago.

9

Internment

On the Scottish island of Islay, a windswept piece of land south-west of the Mull of Kintyre, in the Port Ellen cemetery there stands a granite headstone. Engraved on it are the words: 'Unknown Italian'. There are other such graves with similar headstones on the islands of Oronsay and Colonsay further north in the Hebrides.

The headstones mark the graves of some of the 446 Italians who died when the liner *Arandora Star* was torpedoed off the north coast of Ireland on 2 July 1940, and whose bodies were washed up on the beaches. At the time of the sinking the *Arandora Star* was serving as a prison ship for the deportation of Italian internees and German Jewish refugees to internment camps in Canada. In all 720 men lost their lives on that ship, 446 Italians, 156 Germans and 79 British soldiers. That disaster was the biggest loss of life ever suffered by Italian civilians in a single incident outside their own homeland.

The tragedy is made all the more poignant because the dead were all male civilians ranging in age from 16 to 70, and there were very few Italian families in Scotland that did not suffer a bereavement. At the outbreak of war there were approximately 4000 Italian nationals registered in Scotland, of all ages and genders, which means that there were probably about 1000 Italian families resident here. Fifty-one men who were arrested from these families died on the *Arandora Star*. The names of those who went down with that ship sound like a roll call of the Italian families in Scotland. From Edinburgh, there were the names Crolla, Demarco, Pacitti, Paolozzi (father of Sir Eduardo Paolozzi the sculptor), Coppola, Di Ciacca, Di Rollo, Pelosi and Rossi. From Glasgow, among the dead were: Angiolini, Biagotti, Bertolini, Da Prato, Di Ciacca, Di Luca, Farnocchi, Ferrari, Ghiloni, Gonella, Moscardini, Marsella, Paleschi, Pinchera, Camillo, Agostini, Angiolino and Biagoni; from Ayr: Mancini, Biagi, Filippi, Pieroni and Rossi; Cosomini from Bellshill, Moretti of Greenock, Marzella and Cocozza of Wishaw, Conti of Cowdenbeath, Fortura of Forfar, Ferri of Montrose, Rocchiccioli of Troon,

Santini of Paisley and Fusco of Dundee. Some families had all their males drowned, fathers and sons and brothers.

The *Arandora Star*, a Blue Star cruise liner of 15,500 tons, was one of the four prison ships used for the transportation of prisoners of war and internees from Britain to Canada and Australia. The other three were the *Ettrick,* the *Dunera* and the *Duchess of York*. In this connection, the question arises as to the legality of such a procedure as far as the civilian internees were concerned. The Geneva Convention lays down certain rules regarding the treatment of prisoners of war, but is less specific as to the treatment of enemy civilians. However, one of the provisions of the Geneva document states that civilian internees must be protected from bodily harm and must not be transported across active war zones. If the U-boat-infested seas separating Britain from Canada and Australia were not war zones then how else could they be described?

On 1 July 1940, the *Arandora Star* docked at Liverpool, where she was loaded to capacity with approximately 1673 men. Beside her at the dock was another vessel, the 11,000-ton troopship *Ettrick*, just launched at Glasgow, and later to be sunk on 15 November 1942 by the German submarine U-155 west of Gibraltar. As far as Government reports go, the human cargo of the *Arandora Star* consisted of 743 Italian internees, 479 German-Jewish refugees, and 86 German POWs, but the exact figure is not known, since the method of loading simply consisted of packing as many men aboard as possible until all spaces were full, and no proper records were made. On board also were 174 crew, and a military guard of about 200 soldiers. This was the scene at Liverpool as the ship was being loaded:

'The train journey into the Liverpool dock area did not take long. The carriages drew into a dockside loading area, and we were made to walk a short distance onto a long quay to join other groups already assembled there. Running the length of the pier and towering over the loading sheds, a large, dull, grey ship lay at anchor. We faced the stern of the vessel and on the rear deck, above the name *Arandora Star,* I could see what seemed to be coils of wire with the outline of a large gun behind them. I looked anxiously around me. Packed tightly on the quayside were thousands of men lined up 8 deep the full length of the ship, some standing, some squatting and leaning against each other, some young, some old, and all with a weary resigned look about them. Rows of armed soldiers stood guard around us. After what seemed to be an interminable time, orders were shouted out and the crowd began moving onto a gangway leading up to the ship, urged on by the shouts and the shoves of the soldiers. Since there was only a single gangplank, the loading of the ship proved to be a slow and lengthy process, but when the group still ahead of me was reduced to about 200 men, the ship appeared to have been filled to capacity and the gangway was withdrawn.

By this time our group had been joined by many hundreds of other prisoners. Most were civilians, but many of the newly arrived contingent wore military uniforms which identified them as German soldiers. Some were in Luftwaffe uniform, some wore the dark blue outfits of marine commandos and all looked tired and weary. Most seemed unhurt, but some who wore bandages seemed incapable of standing upright and sat on the ground, leaning against the legs of their compatriots. We learned subsequently that there were 900 of these military personnel. Some were Luftwaffe airmen shot down over southern England and France, but the majority of them were marines captured at the time of the British raids on Stavanger and Narvik in Norway. So we sat and stood and waited and watched as the *Arandora Star* drew away, and wondered what our fate was to be.'

The *Arandora Star* sailed from Liverpool on the afternoon of 1 July and followed a route which brought her north past the Isle of Man, through the North Channel between the Mull of Kintyre and Northern Ireland, past Malin Head, then due west into the open Atlantic. At approximately 1.30am on 2 July, Gunther Prien, German U-boat commander, caught sight of the vessel in his periscope. Gunther Prien was the same commander who, on 14 October, 1939, during the very first weeks of the war, had breached the supposedly impregnable defences at Scapa Flow in the Orkney Islands, and had torpedoed and sunk the battleship *Royal Oak* there.

As his log book later was to show, he was returning to base from a tour of duty in the North Atlantic, with just one torpedo remaining in the submarine's arsenal. His instruments had alerted him to the presence of a ship in his vicinity, and as he surveyed the *Arandora Star* through his periscope, he noted that the unmarked British vessel carried armaments fore and aft and was pursuing an irregular evasive course. He launched his last torpedo at her. It struck in the boiler-room area in the aft region of the ship, and within 30 minutes the *Arandora Star* sank to the bottom of the sea, taking about 720 souls with her. The full extent of the losses will never be known, because the haphazard method of loading did not make for accuracy of count, but the official casualty list showed that 446 Italians, 156 Germans and 79 Britons died.

At about 2.30pm, the Canadian destroyer *HMCS St Laurent* arrived at the scene and began pulling the survivors out of the water. Some were in life-boats, others were lying on improvised rafts. They had been floating on the cold waters of the Atlantic for the better part of 14 hours, but the masses of oil floating on the water had put a layer of insulation on their bodies and had probably saved their lives by preventing the escape of body heat. A Jewish survivor describes the scene:

'The water was full of oil and I hung on to a big piece of wood floating beside me and after a while I managed to pull myself on to it. Hundreds of planks and pieces of wood spiked with barbed wire floated on the water and scraped my skin. There was a slight fog and a drizzly rain and the sea was calm with no wind. I could hear shouts for help in all languages Italian, German, English and Hebrew but these grew less and less as people began to die. I realized that the oil was helping to keep me warm and I tried to cover myself as much as possible with the stuff. Hours later we were pulled out by a Canadian destroyer and we were given hot chocolate to drink and blankets to cover ourselves. All those who needed medical attention were cared for by the ship's doctor, who did his best to help us. The officers and crew on the destroyer treated us well and I would like to thank them for their kindness.'

Rando Bertoia, a young 19-year-old from Glasgow, was fortunate enough to be on a part of the deck not encased in wire when the torpedo struck. He found himself on one of the few lifeboats which had been launched clear of the sinking ship and was witness to the harrowing scenes described above. He was taken aboard by the same destroyer, and from Greenock was taken immediately to Liverpool to be embarked on the ship *Dunera* for transportation to the camps in Australia. Rando, now 84 years of age, still practises his craft as a watchmaker in Glasgow, and is the last living Italian survivor of the sinking of the *Arandora Star*.

The destroyer reached Greenock on the morning of 3 July, and there the survivors were put into three different groups. The sick and the injured were taken to Mearnskirk hospital, where they were treated as ordinary patients. The Italians and the Germans were then separated, and the Italians were marched off from the quay to a factory some hundreds of yards away. No blankets were available and no food was given until that afternoon, when each was given some bread and corned beef and tea. There was no water for washing and the lavatory facilities consisted of two lavatories for about 250 men. The prisoners slept that night as best they could, then next morning they were marched off to another building nearby where they were showered and issued with dry warm clothing. They were then escorted under guard on to a train, and some hours later they arrived back at Liverpool, where they were marched on to the selfsame dock where they had embarked from from days before. There at anchor was another ship, the *Dunera,* and the weary and shocked prisoners were marched up a gangplank into that ship.

The sinking of the *Arandora Star* and the heavy loss of Italian life raised a furore in the Italian-American population of the USA, and the American Ambassador in London, John Kennedy, father of the future president, with no doubt the Italian-American vote in mind, raised the question as to why the International Red Cross had not been notified of the status of the ship. Lord Snell, the English Peer, raised the same question in the House of Lords, but the rapid developments on the war fronts soon pushed the incident out of the limelight. Thousands of soldiers were being killed and wounded in the retreat to Dunkirk, and the sinking of another ship had to be looked at in that context.

The *Dunera* was a purpose-built troopship of 11,000 tons, with accommodation for 1,000 men. Loaded to almost three times her intended capacity, she left Liverpool on 11 July with 2,546 internees, 200 of them the Italians who had been sunk on the *Arandora Star* just a few days before. She had a crew of 75 and about 200 soldier guards under the command of Lt. Col. Scott. Most of the soldiers had themselves just been released from the detention they had undergone for a variety of charges.

The conditions on board were dreadful. The 'guards' mistreated their prisoners, sometimes brutally. The internees were stripped and searched, all valuables confiscated and all luggage, such as there was, taken away and never returned. Some of it was simply thrown overboard. The prisoners were packed tight into every corner of the ship and there was barely enough room left for them to walk, with barbed wire barricades everywhere. There were no sanitary facilities. Buckets which slopped over with every movement of the ship were placed on the floor of the decks and prisoners on the lower decks were often sprayed with vomit and urine from them. Two days out from

111

Liverpool, the *Dunera* was intercepted by a German submarine, the U-56 under the command of Oberleutnant Harms, who fired three torpedoes at her. Two missed, but the third, which fortunately failed to explode, hit the *Dunera* amidships, and only minor damage was inflicted to the vessel. After 15 days at sea the *Dunera* pulled in at Freetown in Sierra Leone on the west coast of Africa to take in supplies, then continued down to Capetown where several of the ship's crew deserted, taking with them the valuables they had stripped from the prisoners. In all, the journey to Australia lasted 57 days, and many of the prisoners hardly saw the light of day in all that time.

The Australian authorities in Melbourne, the port of arrival, were appalled at the conditions they saw on the ship, and a report was sent back to London describing the dreadful state of the ship and of the prisoners. Questions were asked in Parliament, and an investigation was carried out, and as a result Lieutenant Colonel Scott was court-martialed and severely reprimanded. The prisoners were unloaded from the *Dunera* and taken to converted ware-houses at the dockside which had been fitted out for the arrival of the prison-ers. There they were deloused and showered, given a medical examination, and provided with fresh clothing to replace the filthy rags they had been wearing for the past two months. The Italians were separated from the Germans, then taken by train to the Tatura region, where a camp had been prepared for the arrival of prisoners.

Tatura was one of the many POW and internment camps scattered throughout Australia and located far from any city, so that the prisoners could not have contact with Australian civilians. Although in the middle of the wilderness, the camp was spacious and well-equipped, with plenty of open ground between the huts which served as living quarters, and all the other facilities, latrines, showers and well-stocked first aid huts, at a distance from them. The kitchens and eating quarters were also separate from the sleeping areas, and the Australian authorities were careful to adhere rigidly to the terms of the Geneva Convention and to ensure the safety and well-being of all prisoners, regardless of status. The civilian camps were supervised by only a handful of guards, since escape was looked upon as a very remote possibil-ity, given the vast distances which separated the camp from any centre of population. To relieve the inevitable boredom and depression brought about by long periods within the confines of the compound, prisoners were in-vited to work on nearby farms. It was not unknown for prisoners working on these work parties to fall asleep under the shade of a tree. When they awoke to find themselves in a deserted field they would make their own way back to the camp and bang on the gates for entry. With the hot, harsh country that surrounded them, few were inclined to consider escape, for there was simply nowhere to escape to. All kinds of social activities were encouraged and those prisoners who elected to work outside the compound received the equivalent of one shilling and sixpence per day, with which they could buy cigarettes and chocolates in the camp canteens.

When the *Dunera* Italians arrived, this camp already had a population of twenty-eight internees, all of them Russians who had been farming in the Melbourne district. White Russians, the guards called them, because of their anti-communist politics. They were uncommunicative, kept themselves strictly to themselves and made no effort to make contact with the newly arrived Italians. The guards were strict but perfectly proper in the treatment of the prisoners and the food was plentiful and of the same quality as that given to the Australian army soldiers who guarded them. To the prisoners, dulled into resignation by a succession of traumatic and seemingly never-ending shocks, the Tatura camp was akin to paradise.

Discipline in this particular camp became lax to the extent that some of the prisoners were able to set up a still for the manufacture of a potent alcoholic beverage, distilled from sultanas and all kinds of grain brought in for kitchen use. This was distributed free throughout the camp to those of their colleagues who enjoyed a tipple, but their generosity did not extend to the guards, who had to pay for the pleasure of sampling the camp rotgut. The camp authorities were forced to come down hard on this practice after an incident which caused a mild furore. Four prisoners had to be taken to a hospital in Melbourne, a journey of nearly two days given the slowness of the train and the frequent stops in sidings on the single-track railway. The prisoners were under the guard of a young soldier who was supposed to stand guard with rifle and bayonet over his charges. A combination of heat and boredom made him accept gratefully an occasional swig from a prisoner's canteen, which had been filled at the camp with some of the day's production from the still. On arrival in Melbourne, the detail sent to escort the party to the hospital found the young soldier asleep, with his loaded rifle being cared for by the prisoners he was supposed to be guarding. The Australian army reaction to this incident can well be imagined.

Given the laxity of the guards, escape from the camp was easy but pointless, with the desert wilderness all around. However, never a day passed but what some prisoners would decide to slip under the barbed wire and go for a walk in the bush, simply for want of something better to do. Sometimes the absence would last for a day or two, but the fugitive would invariably return to the camp, his desire for a little freedom exhausted. These escapades would be punished by a spell in the detention cells, where the prisoner could eat and drink to his heart's content, thus making up for the deprivations imposed by his walk in the countryside. At the end of the war Italian and German prisoners were encouraged to remain as settlers in Australia, and many without family ties in their homeland did so rather than return to their devastated homes. There were about a dozen camps in all, scattered all over Australia: at Marrinup, Parkeston and Woodmans Point. These sites are now much visited by amateur archaeologists, often the descendants of prisoners once housed there, in a search for wartime tokens and badges.

If the possibility of escape did not come into consideration as far as the Australian camps were concerned, because of their remoteness, the same did not apply to the camp on St Helene's Island in Canada. The USA, only 40 miles away, was still neutral during the first year of the war, and freedom could be found there for those brave enough to attempt an escape across the St Lawrence River. The prisoners were inspired by the story of Lt Franz Von Werra and his incredible escape from Canada and eventual return to Germany. His story had been told and retold in the Canadian POW camps, reaching legendary status in the telling, and had inspired many would-be fugitives. In later years the story of his escape was to be told in a Hollywood film 'The One That Got Away', with Hardy Kruger in the part of Von Werra.

Von Werra had become something of a cult figure amongst the prisoners in Camp 43, and a handful of reckless prisoners had tried to emulate his feat, but had never got more than a few hundred yards from the compound. Their attempts had only gone to increase the already strict discipline and surveillance the prisoners were subjected to.

These strict measures were not applied in the case of George Barletta, a quiet, unobtrusive 30-year-old tailor who had lived and worked in Edinburgh since his arrival from Italy about 15 years before. A reserved and uncomplaining bachelor with few friends, he had acquired the repuation amongst the guards as being a quiet, docile and willing worker who never gave trouble. He volunteered daily for the work parties, for he enjoyed the occasional hard physical labour involved in clearing shrubs and bushes, the felling of trees and the maintenance of the many paths and walkways on the island.

Because of his reputation Barletta was chosen daily for these work parties, and in time had got to know the geography of the island thoroughly. On one occasion he was given the task of clearing out a storage hut at the edge of a remote clearing, where he was left to his own resources by a trusting guard. He was told to join the main group of prisoners when summoned by the whistle which signalled the end of the shift. In a corner of the hut, half-hidden under a pile of old workclothes and assorted lumber, Barletta came across a rusty old bicycle. The machine, though covered in dust and cobwebs, seemed in fair enough condition and he spent some time cleaning and oiling it with some lubricant which he found close by. The tyres seemed firm enough, so he began to pedal slowly and thoughtfully round the clearing, nursing the germ of an exciting thought.

That night, putting his tailoring skills to work, he removed the broad red stripe from his POW trousers and the red circle from the back of his POW jacket, and replaced them with patches of blue material so as to make a normal-looking suit, then loosely stitched back the red prisoner patches into place. Next day, he went out with the work party again and was assigned another solitary task. He waited until the guard had gone, stripped off the red markings, ran to the clearing where the bicycle had been left and proceeded to pedal casually towards the slip-road leading to the bridge. He waved to the guards on duty, who paid no attention to the civilian passing by on a bike, and then pedaled furiously over the bridge and into the city of Montreal across the river.

There he spent an idyllic morning, alternately pedaling and walking his bicycle along the broad Montreal avenues, drinking in the sights and sounds of freedom. Taking careful note of the passage of time, he made his way back to the river, pedaled on to the bridge towards the island, where he joined the slip-road down, waving cheerfully to the guards as he did so, who again paid no attention to the civilian on a bike. Arriving back at his departure point in the clearing, he replaced the bicycle in the hut, fixed the red markings back onto his clothes, and minutes later, summoned by the assembly whistle, re-joined his group to be counted and escorted back to the camp. Next day he repeated the procedure. He explored a different part of the city, enjoying to the full the sensation of unhindered and unlimited movement, taking care to be back on the island in time for the guard's count.

On the third day disaster struck. He had gone as far as the summit of Mount Royal and had sat a while at the base of the huge cross, admiring the view down over the city to the river and the bridge, until it was time to go back. He mounted the bicycle and pushed off, freewheeling down the gentle slope of the hill, when, without any warning, his front wheel collapsed in a tangle of wire spokes and struts, throwing him heavily to the ground. Shaken but unhurt, he started off on foot towards the island, for with not a cent in his pocket to pay for any form of transport, he was left with a long walk back to the island, with no possibility of being on time for roll-call.

The guard in charge of the work party counted and recounted his prison-ers, but at last had to accept the fact that he was a man short. The alarm was given, the guard at the bridge trebled, and news of the escape, together with a description of the fugitive, was given to the Montreal police.

About two hours later a footsore Barletta arrived at the Jacques Cartier bridge, squared his shoulders, then began the long trek over the pedestrian walkway towards the island and on to the slip-road leading down to the fort. He noticed the trebling of the guard and the armoured vehicles with guns at the ready, who took only casual notice of the pedestrian walking along to-wards the island, for their orders were to stop anyone leaving the area, not going towards it. Barletta was soon back in his clearing, where the red mark-ings were waiting to be replaced on his prison uniform.

Up he marched to the fortress gates, rattled the bars and demanded entry of a startled guard who escorted him immediately to the officer in charge of the search. The latter listened somewhat sceptically to his tale of having fallen asleep under a bush and only just awakened; the scepticism turning to complete disbelief when the superimposed red markings on his clothes were noticed. So Barletta told the truth, although this too was rejected as being very improbable, until the Montreal police reported finding a damaged bicy-cle on the slopes of Mount Royal. Whilst the episode could hardly be classi-fied as an escape, it did earn him the acclamation and respect of his fellow prisoners, together with the usual 30 days in the punishment cells.

To a very large extent the treatment of the internees in the Canadian and Australian camps depended on the character and disposition of the officers and soldiers set to guard them, and under the command of humane officers even the very worst of conditions were made bearable and the personal prop-erty of prisoners was safeguarded by conscientious officials. To illustrate this we have to go back to an incident in the wartime experiences of the Martinez family mentioned in the previous chapter.

Giuseppe Martinez, who had collaborated in the invention of the degaussing cable for the neutralizing of magnetic mines, had another son, George, who had recently graduated from Cambridge. He too was arrested at the outbreak of war with Italy, but was separated from his father and brother on the docks at Liver-pool and loaded onto the second ship to leave, the *Ettrick*, and found himself in Camp 43 on St Helene's Island on the St Lawrence river. A few weeks before Mussolini's declaration of war, George had become engaged to Mariolina Antonucci, the daughter of a colonel in the Italian army. Soon after her en-gagement she went to visit her father, who was in command of a unit stationed in Jimma, a small town some miles south-west of Addis Ababa in Ethiopia.

No sooner had she arrived than war broke out, and there she remained until the town was captured by the British on 6 April 1941. The final defeat of the Italian Army at Keren some weeks later signalled the collapse of Italian resistance in Africa, and all Italian civilians in Ethiopia were rounded up and interned. Together with some others, Miss Antonucci was taken to an internment camp in Madera, an outpost in Somaliland, where she was stripped of all her personal jewellery and valuables. She had no knowledge of the fate of her fiancé George, nor he of hers. Indeed, the remaining Martinez family in Naples (George's mother and one other brother) were convinced that all the family had perished on the *Arandora Star*. It was not until almost a year after the sinking of that ship that the family were put in touch with one another through the International Red Cross. After several more months Miss Antonucci was repatriated and, overjoyed at the news of her fiancé's survival, wrote him a letter through the Red Cross with all her news. Incensed at hearing of Mariolina's treatment and loss, with his Camp Commandant's permission George wrote to the Home Office in London stating the facts of the case and complained bitterly about the loss of her personal valuables. In due time he received a polite acknowledgement of the letter from a Home Office official.

The war ended, George and Mariolina married and settled down in Romsey in the south of England, where he again took up his career. Some months later in 1947 a neatly-packed parcel was delivered to them. Inside it, and none the worse for wear, were all the valuables and jewels taken from Mariolina in Ethiopia in April 1941! There is probably no other army and civil service in the world who could have been so meticulous, in the middle of a desperate war, in the safeguarding of property belonging to an enemy alien.

At the beginning of the war, hotels and boarding houses on the Isle of Man were commandeered by the Government and were fenced in with barbed wire to serve as internment camps. This was the same procedure used in the First World War, when the Isle of Man served as an internment island for German enemy aliens. The Italians who were fortunate enough to have missed transportation to Canada and Australia on the *Ettrick*, the *Arandora Star* and the *Dunera*, were taken to the Isle of Man and housed in the Metropole Hotel in Ochan and the Palace and the Granville in Ramsey. Conditions in these camps were good, with plenty of space and sanitary facilities for the internees, and for those who cared to, work was available on neighbouring farms. Lorries would load up each morning with volunteers to be deposited at various farms throughout the island and picked up again to be returned to their camp in the evening. The food was adequate and no different from the rations of any wartime Briton, and those who worked on the farms could pick up extra delicacies such as eggs and milk from the farmers. Generally speaking, the farmers found these internees to be good and willing workers, whilst the prisoners were glad to be free of the constricting environment of the wire-enclosed hotels. Visits from families were allowed as far as the limited wartime transportation permitted, and one letter a week could be written to family or friends. Canteens which sold cigarettes, soft drinks and as much chocolate as the limited war-time rationing allowed were run by the prisoners themselves, who were allowed the use of their own money to buy such-like comforts.

The camps on the Isle of Man were to a very large extent self-ruled by the internees, with a minimum of interference on the part of the soldier guards. A camp leader was elected from one of their own colleagues by the prisoners, a spokesman whose duty it was to ensure that the orders of the military as far as the general running of the camp was concerned were carried out, and who could complain to the authorities on the internees' behalf if necessary. Prisoners were quartered two to a room, and each morning a roll call and inspection was carried out by the soldiers in charge. Rations were delivered to the camps each day, and since there was no shortage of chefs and cooks among the prisoners, some of them from the best hotels and restaurants in London, the best possible use was made of the food provided, and although these rations were the same as were issued to the soldier guards, the prisoners were invariably presented with a far better meal from the same raw materials. A section of each hotel was set aside as hospital quarters for the sick, and the local hospital was available for emergencies.

The Onchan camp acted as a transit camp for prisoners repatriated from Camp 43 in Montreal, who began to arrive back to the UK in late 1943 after Italy's capitulation, at which time they had ceased to be enemy aliens. They arrived at the Isle of Man camp in small groups whenever transportation was available on the convoys of ships from Canada. These 'Canadians', as they were called by the inmates of Onchan, who had spent more than 3 years in the cramped and spartan confines of the fortress on St Helene's Island and subjected to the rigorous regime in force there, were amazed at the quality of the accommodation available to their fellow internees. They were amazed too at the comparative freedom and absence of rigid discipline afforded to those of their fellow citizens who had been lucky enough to escape the prison ships and transportation overseas. The internees who were sent to the Isle of Man received good, humane and proper treatment at the hands of their captors, as befitted their status as civilians. This cannot be said of their colleagues who were transported to Canada on the prison ship *Ettrick* to be interned in Camp 43 on St Helene's island in Montreal. This is a description of the reception they encountered on their arrival at that camp after 13 days on board the *Ettrick:*

'Clutching our belongings, all 407 of us stumbled awkwardly down the gangplank. Those who had never moved from the confines of the hold were half-blinded by the unaccustomed sunlight, but those who could gazed around in wonder at our new surroundings. The scent of flowers and shrubs and fresh air was immediately appreciated by everyone. As we came down the gangplank, one by one, our names were taken by Captain Vinden, and we then assembled on the quayside which was tightly ringed by armed soldiers and military vehicles. We presented a sorry sight. For a month now we had lived and slept in the same clothes, and only the most rudimentary hygiene had been possible. Many had not shaved for weeks, and as we stood in clothes stained with vomit and excrement, lice-ridden and scratching, a more unkempt and dirty bunch would have been hard to imagine.

We sat and waited on the dock for some time, looking at the magnificent vistas of Quebec around us. Then, in response to the orders of the captain, we began to shuffle out of the dock area through a gauntlet of soldiers. Orders were given in an almost incomprehensible English-French patois, the meaning of which was plain enough when accompanied by the butt-end of a rifle. A huge Canadian Pacific train had got up steam by the dockside and we climbed into it as our suitcases and belongings were snatched away unceremoniously in the process. As we got on each man was issued with a large brown paper bag, which, to our delight, contained a welcome and unexpected surprise. Inside was the whitest of white bread, cheese, fruit, tins of tuna fish, little pats of butter and miniature jars of jam and marmalade. Whoops of joy greeted the discovery, and elation spread contagiously throughout the prisoners. We reacted like children who had just been given surprise bags of sweets. As we settled down to our new surroundings, Captain Vinden limped through the carriages, which were of an open type strange to our eyes. In each one he made a short statement to the effect that the food just issued had to last two days and thus was to be rationed accordingly. Then he disappeared, not to be seen again for two eventful days.

The train set off to the sound of almost hysterical song and merriment. Having eaten and enjoyed some of the food, for my appetite was now beginning to return, I settled back comfortably to enjoy the unfolding majesty of the Canadian scenery. The train puffed steadily through villages and hamlets with strange-sounding French names: Pont Rouge, Deshamboult, Trois Rivières, and as the day went on speculation mounted as to our possible destination. Night had fallen when the train drew up in what was obviously a large city, and the name Montreal spread rapidly through the carriages. A small fleet of buses and military vehicles had drawn up beside the train, and we were given orders to move out. It seemed we had finally arrived at our destination.

Holding on tightly to our precious food parcels, we began to file out of the carriages, laughing and joking amongst ourselves and shouting pleasantries at the impassive guards who stood with rifles and bayonets at the ready at the exit to each compartment. Chattering excitedly to my companions and holding my food parcel firmly, I jumped up the few steps onto one of the buses. In the back were three guards. When 20 men were loaded into each vehicle three more guards were positioned at the exit and the doors closed. In all there were 20 buses, and all were being loaded in the same manner. The fleet of vehicles then moved off, preceded by some sort of military half-track with a machine-gun mounted on the rear. Glancing back, I could see a similar armoured car making up the rear of the convoy.

The vehicles made their way along the brightly lit streets of the city, with policemen at each intersection ensuring an unhindered passage for the convoy. We carried on through quieter streets until we reached the massive spans of a huge steel girder bridge. As I looked down from it, a cluster of intense bright lights under the far end of the bridge a hundred yards or so away caught my eye. The buses slowed to a crawl, and I could see about 80 feet below us a small rectangular area flooded in the glare of powerful searchlights. There were uniformed figures moving around in front of a long, low, building of some sort, and as the buses reached the end of the bridge to begin a slow descent, the lights disappeared from view, leaving only a bright glow in the sky. Slowly the convoy moved on, and finally came to a halt in front of a set of iron gates flanked on either side by the pillars of a massive stone archway. The leading armoured car slowly preceded the first bus through the gates, followed by the second bus, then after a short interval, by the third. It was then our turn, and the bus jerked forward and stopped after a few yards. A blinding light shone into the interior, the door flew open, the three guards at the front jumped out, and a blast of sound erupted into the bus.

'*Heraus! Heraus! Schnell!* Out!', and, suddenly frightened, we descended from the bus, urged on by the three guards at the rear.

I paused at the top of the step, blinded by the dazzling light in my eyes. A hand reached out, grabbed the lapel of my jacket and pulled me sprawling to the ground. I tried to get up. Another set of hands pulled at my food parcel. Instinctively I held on and pulled back. A truncheon smashed into my forearm, forcing me to release my grip and I fell to my knees, impelled forward by a blow to my back. Dazed and shaken I was hauled to my feet by two soldiers shouting at me in German.

'*Schnell! Schnell!*'

I was dragged forward several steps, then with a rifle-butt blow to my back, I was forced to the ground in a squatting position. This procedure was repeated as each unsuspecting prisoner stepped down. Some fared better than others, but everyone had their food parcels clubbed from them and all of were pushed, rifle-butted, and kicked to a squatting position on the ground while the guards continued their verbal tirade. The priests fared worse of all, for the sight of their habit seemed to spur the guards to even greater effort, and the six unfortunates were clubbed and kicked unmercifully, their clothes all but torn from their backs.

As each bus entered, the focus of attention was drawn further away from our group and I sat rigid with fear, trying to summon up enough courage inconspicuously to angle my head slightly to observe our surroundings. There were three groups of prisoners before ours already sitting on the ground, each with four soldiers standing over them menacingly. Clearly each group had been greeted in the same way as ours, for they were all bruised, their clothes torn and bloodstained. We were sitting in some kind of courtyard, and as my eyes became accustomed to the glare of the searchlights I made out the outline of the long, low building in the background. Curious as I was to see behind me, I did not dare move my head for fear of another blow, but from the corner of my eye I could make out a high wooden platform. On it was a machine-gun manned by a soldier. My stomach grew cold with fear. Armed soldiers paraded up and down in front of us, and paused occasionally to fire shots into the air. Half a dozen huge Alsatian dogs roamed in and out of the squatting men, sniffing and barking furiously and adding to the general air of intimidation. If all this had been meant to cow and frighten, then the plan had succeeded very well indeed, for we sat petrified with terror, and the thought passed through my mind that this could very well be our last moment on earth.

Some in the group were crying quietly, some were repeating Hail Marys under their breath, some were cursing quietly. Jimmy Berretti, a tall, quiet youngster from Ayr, was shivering uncontrollably despite the warmth of the night, and I could feel nausea and panic begin to well up inside me. Sitting cross-legged in front of me was Ronnie Girasole, my cellmate at the time of my arrest. One of the marauding dogs stopped beside him and peed on his leg. 'Fuckin' bastards... fuckin' bastards!' was his angry whisper, at which my growing panic turned into a semi-hysterical giggle. The unloading and manhandling took the better part of two hours, and when completed we were in 20 groups of 20 frightened men sitting on the ground, fearfully and passively awaiting whatever else might be in store for us. A Canadian officer approached the first group and began to shout at them in a staccato flow of German. Enraged at the lack of response, he repeated himself even louder, and poked his stick at one of the prisoners in front of him. Ralph Taglione, who until his arrest had managed Quaglino's well-known restaurant in London, one side of his face badly swollen from a blow, raised a hesitant hand and spoke in a cultivated English accent.

'Please sir... nobody here speaks German.'

The officer looked at him blankly. 'What do you mean you don't speak German? What bloody language do you speak?'

'Please sir, everybody here speaks English.'

'English?', the officer seemed confused. 'What do you mean English? Where do you come from?'

'Please sir, in this group we are all Italians from London.'

The officer's jaw sagged slightly. He looked oddly at Taglione, then turned on his heels to confer with a major standing close by. The major listened, then motioned to Taglione, who stood up and hobbled over to the him, barely able to walk. He questioned the London Italian closely, and I could see him listening intently to the Londoner's answers. These were long and fluent, punctuated by a series of gestures, ending with a characteristic arms half-raised, palms upturned, hunched shoulders pose which spoke volumes.

It will probably never be possible to discover the combination of events which brought 407 Italian internees to a camp obviously prepared for high-risk Nazis, and the truth of the matter will probably remain unknown forever to those who suffered that night. Was the sinking of the *Arandora Star* a factor? Had the camp been prepared for the Germans who sailed on *that* ship? But the Germans on the *Arandora Star,* with the exception of the 86 soldier POWs, were all Jewish or political refugees, who no more merited the treatment of that first night than we Italians did. Were the priests singled out for special treatment because it was thought that they were spies disguised as priests? Why were the soldiers' commands given in German? Why were all the notices in the compound written in that language? The camp had obviously been specifically prepared for an intake of German POWs such as the *Ettrick* had carried. Could there have been a mix-up at Quebec, with our group sent off to the wrong destination?

But Captain Vinden knew the truth about the men whose names he had read out in Warth Mills some two weeks before. He certainly knew their nationality, so why had the colonel in charge of the reception of the prisoners, who was obviously convinced that he was dealing with Germans, not been informed of their true identity?

What is certain is that no one, least of all a bunch of hapless internees consisting of boys, old men, shopkeepers, waiters, chefs, doctors, refugees and deckhands should have been subjected to the calculated brutalities of that night. And all for having committed the crime of being born an Italian or possessing an Italian name. That no one was killed or seriously injured is remarkable, and the memory of the first night at Camp S will long remain in the minds of those who experienced it.'

Camp 43 on St Helene's Island on the St Lawrence river facing Montreal, where the Italians from the *Ettrick* were decanted, was a completely different proposition from the hotels on the Isle of Man. The accommodation prepared for them was inside a grim fortress built on a slope by the St Lawrence river in 1611 by Champlain, the first governor of French Canada. The massive stone building had been encircled by high barbed wire fences to form a prison camp and consisted of a long three-sided structure of three floors, built of stone blocks about two feet thick. Across the front of the building a seven-foot-high, double barbed-wire fence had been erected to form a courtyard about 100ft wide by 350ft long. At either end of the fence stood an elevated wooden tower, each equipped with a heavy machine-gun manned by three soldiers. The whole structure ran parallel to the river, separated from it by some 50 yards of gently sloping ground. Across the river lay the city of Montreal, surmounted by a huge neon illuminated crucifix on the heights of Mount Royal beyond. Dominating the scene was the impressive structure of the Jacques Cartier bridge as it passed over the northern end of the building, with one of its giant concrete pylons almost touching the perimeter fence of the compound. The old fortress of Ste Hélène, built 300 years ago by Champlain on the island named after his young bride, was now serving as an internment camp for 407 Italian prisoners.

In complete contrast to the conditions on the Isle of Man, the place was run like a high-security prison. Armed guards patrolled up and down the outside length of the barbed wire fence, and the machine guns on either side of the courtyard were constantly manned, each by two soldiers. The rag-tag mixture of young boys, old men, waiters, café and fish and chip shop owners and priests could not have been better guarded had they been a regiment of Hitler's elite SS troops. Two-tiered bunk beds, no more than 3 feet apart on either side of narrow low tunnel-like rooms, served as sleeping accommodation, and for sanitary arrangements 20 lavatory seats at one end of the building had to make do for the 400 persons there. Discipline was strict, and any infringement of the rules could result in a sojourn in one of the three detention cells at one end of the building. One redeeming feature was the excellent quality of the food available, far superior in quantity, variety and quality than could have been dreamed of in a rationed Britain, and which, as was the case in the Isle of Man camps, was prepared by some of the best London chefs. Work parties were not the informal unsupervised affairs they were on the Isle of Man; those volunteering for any kind of work outside the camp gates were accompanied by armed guards almost as numerous as the docile prisoners they were guarding. Even when it became obvious to the camp authorities that what had come to them from the *Ettrick* was only a bunch of harmless civilians, the rigour of the camp routine was scarcely relaxed and discipline was kept as severe as ever.

Medical facilities were rudimentary and consisted of four beds set up in a small storeroom which was euphemistically labeled as a hospital. There was one doctor among the prisoners, a Dr Rybekil, a Londoner whose origins lay in the extreme north of Italy and who spoke little or no Italian. He went by the name of Dr Aspirin, since that was the only drug available for him to dispense. Fortunately the prisoners were in the main young and healthy, and his limited resources were only once put to the test. He suspected a case of tuberculosis in one of the prisoners, and had the Camp Leader insist that a doctor be called in from a Montreal hospital, who confirmed the diagnosis. This was at the beginning of November, the start of the Canadian winter, and to serve as an isolation ward a tent was pitched in a corner of the court-yard, with a charcoal fire for heat, and there the poor unfortunate spent the next three months, a lone blanket-wrapped figure seated inside his tent with the temperature outside plunging at times as low as minus 30 degrees. Apart from Dr Rybekil, who at times sat with his patient for hours, no-one went near the man. He was shunned as if smitten by the plague, which in a sense indeed he was. He was finally transferred to a city hospital to face an unknown fate.

For a few months in 1942 the camp housed a local Canadian celebrity, Mayor Houde of Montreal. The French-Canadian mayor of that city was arrested for advocating that no French-Canadian should enlist in the army to fight an English war which had nothing to do with the Quebecois. He was housed under guard in one of the three detention cells, then taken to a Canadian internment camp in Sherbrooke further along the St Lawrence.

Without being aware of it and without necessarily wanting to, the 407 docile and harmless Italian civilian internees on St Helene's Island were performing a great service for the Axis war effort. For three years the guarding of them in Camp 43 kept tied down scores of Canadian fighting men whose presence in any of the war zones might have measurably shortened the war.

The youth of modern Italy are beginning to take a new interest in the events of those wartime days, the truth of which was distorted by the fascist government, and later also by the Allies for reasons of popular propaganda. The first casualty in war is truth, and the truth of long-past events is hard to come by. Each observer or participant has his own view and his own interpretation of the facts. A journalist, Bernabei, has this to write about the sinking of the *Arandora Star* in an article which appeared recently in the newspaper *L'Unita* entitled 'The Forgotten Tragedy'.

'All this was the result of Churchill's order 'Collar the lot', when asked who amongst the Italians had to be arrested. All males between 17 and 70 were ordered to be arrested, but the arrests were much more indiscriminate; boys of 14 and old men of eighty found themselves behind barbed wire and in the bowels of prison ships taking them to Canada and Australia. 1,500 civilians were shipped abroad in this way, all indiscriminately arrested without regard to age or political affiliation. All arrests were arbitrary. They were Italians. That was enough. The lists for internment were drawn up by bureaucrats whose function it was to draw up lists to meet a predetermined quota. There comes to mind Colonel Kappler of the SS, who had to spend a night making up a list of 320 villagers to be executed in the Ardeatine Caves as a reprisal for the killing of some German soldiers. For each German who died, a multiple of Italians had to die. There comes to mind also the famous list of communists, never seen by anyone, but believed in by everyone, waved by Senator McCarthy as proof of the infiltration of Communists into America.

These are all disasters of civilisation. Permits can be issued, persons can be incriminated, deported, killed, in a rational and orderly impersonal manner. Somewhere a line has to be drawn and decisions are arbitrarily made. A 'Mason–Dixon Line' is drawn in America, what does it separate? A different shade of earth, different types of behaviour? Does intolerance cease north of this imaginary line? Does the possession of an Italian name make that person worthy of incarceration? Must all those who took their holidays in Italy become suspect? Italy is the aggressor. Britain has the right to defend itself of course. What does a British civil servant, accustomed to strictly logical conclusions, do in such circumstances? How can he differentiate between the good and the bad, and how does he satisfy the demands of his superiors? The bottom line is that a list of names makes order out of chaos, fills the *Arandora Star* and the Ardeatine Caves and satisfies the McCarthyites. What matters is the list, not what it contains. In the sinking of the *Arandora Star* Decio Anzani dies. He was the Secretary of the Anti-Fascist Italian League for the Rights of Man and an enemy of the Fascists. But Umberto Limentani, the Fascist lawyer, the formulator in Rome of the anti-Jewish laws of 1938, the arch-enemy of freedom, is not on that list. He does not die; he lives out the war in the comparative luxury of the Isle of Man internment camps.

But there are other and more indistinct lines, yet more shadowy subtleties. In Great Britain, the memory of an injustice done because of prejudice, arrogance and inefficiency asks questions of the conscience of those who believed themselves to be in the right (and who presume to believe themselves to be always in the right).

Here in Italy, the affair did not even touch the national memory. The only thing that remains, the only memory of the dead, is the name of a street in Bardi near Parma, where 48 of the victims came from, then in 1990, the somewhat incongruous title of Cavaliere awarded by our government to all those who survived from that town, as though survival in itself bestowed some merit.'

❉ 10 ❉

Aftermath

Slowly, as the Home Office set up tribunals to examine each individual case and as the harmlessness of the majority of the internees became apparent, most of the prisoners on the Isle of Man were given their freedom and began the return to their homes and families. The release of the younger and fitter internees was granted only on the condition that they took up some form of work of national importance. This could consist of agricultural work, digging for coal in the pits, or any kind of work that would assist the war effort. Then, at the end of 1943 with the defeat of the Axis forces in North Africa, the invasion of Sicily and the fall of Mussolini, Italy ceased to be an enemy nation, the new Italian government under General Badoglio declared itself an ally of Britain and turned to fight against the Germans. So once again, in the space of one day, the status of Italians in Britain changed. No longer were they enemy aliens, they were now allies, and the gates of all the camps, on the Isle of Man, in Canada and in Australia were thrown open to all except the handful of fascist diehards who refused to accept Italy's change of allegiance and who chose to remain in the camps as prisoners.

These are the emotions of one such ex-Italian enemy alien as he returned to his family in Scotland from his captivity in a Canadian camp:

> 'The transition from prisoner status to free man is not easy, however, and to find oneself alone amongst people who until a few hours ago had classified you as an enemy can be a traumatic experience. Together with another 25 prisoners from Camp 43 on St Helene's Island I was declared free by the Home Office and waited for some weeks for space to be available on a ship to return us to our homes in Britain. Even though we were free men, we were put under armed guard and taken by train to Halifax, where we embarked on the *Queen Elizabeth*, now in use as a troopship during the years of war. After a three day journey across the

Atlantic at a speed which made the liner safe from German sub-marines, we were escorted to Onchan Camp on the Isle of Man by two friendly unarmed and elderly members of the Home Guard. There I was given a ferry and railway ticket to Glasgow and left to my own resources. After three years of captivity these were my thoughts and emotions:

I was a now suddenly a completely free man, standing alone in a Liverpool railway station waiting for the Glasgow train. For the first time in three years I was not under some form of mili-tary constraint or other. I was now left completely to my own resources and free to move about as I pleased without any con-straint. The sensation was a strange and frightening one. I could feel anxiety and apprehension well up inside me, and for a brief moment I almost wished I were back in the compound of Camp 43 surrounded by all the well-known and now strangely com-fortable elements of that environment.

Sudden release from captivity can be almost as traumatic as the shock of arrest. The suddenness of my imprisonment had cut me off without warning from my family and friends and the environment I had always known. As a prisoner, the routine duties of having to earn a living and making a way for myself in life had stopped. As a prisoner, life was organised forcibly for me and I no longer had the need to take responsibility for myself. Existence was merely a long round of killing time, obeying or-ders and waiting for an uncertain future, with my destiny no longer in my own hands. For the past three years I simply had to obey my guards and do exactly as I was told and when I was told. I had no personal choice in the way my life was organized and during that time I had become effectively depersonalised. With my release, the tensely wound psychological spring which I had wrapped around myself and which had enabled me to come to terms with my captivity seemed to have suddenly snapped and I was left with a strange feeling of insecurity. I was now free and without constraint, and had to depend purely on my own resources. There was no one there to order me what to do or how to do it, no one at my side to pull at me by the arm or ready to give me a nudge with a rifle butt, no one to tell me when or what I could eat and no armed soldier with rifle at the ready to make sure I obeyed orders.

There were scores of people, most of them in uniform, with me on the platform waiting for the Glasgow train. With a tight aching knot in my stomach I looked around at my neighbours. These were people who for the last three years had looked upon me as a dangerous enemy and had kept me locked away behind barbed wire, I thought to myself. What would their reaction be if they knew who and what I was? How would they react if they knew that until a few weeks ago I had been looked upon as the enemy? I longed for the sight of a familiar face, of a familiar figure to turn and talk to, but there was none, and something akin to panic began to well up within me. There were a few civilians standing about on the platform, but in the main the waiting passengers were military personnel of both sexes, weighed down by their kit, either going on leave or returning to their units. They stood in little groups chatting and laughing and joking, and I felt myself the complete outsider, envious of their camaraderie, alone, isolated, and afraid to engage in conversation with anyone, lest my status be discovered and my identity as an ex-enemy alien made known to all.

In the packed train compartment I politely refused the many offers of cigarettes and sandwiches from my fellow travellers. I fended off their attempts at conversation as non-committally and as politely as I could, and since my accent was Scottish and in no way out of place, I aroused no suspicion among them. Then, so as not to have to participate in their exchange of introductions and jocular small talk, I closed my eyes and pretended to fall asleep. The pretence turned to reality and I did sleep, to be jolted awake by the jerking of the train as it drew into Glasgow's Central Station. It was dark on the platform as I stepped down from the compartment. I had forgotten about the blackout, and in the dim light I did not at first recognise the uniformed figure approaching alongside the train. Slightly more grizzled and greyer than three years before, and now in a police inspector's uniform, was my father's old policeman friend Alex McCrae, the one who had come to arrest me on that fateful night more than three years before. His hand reached out and shook mine.

'So you're back now, Joe. How's it going?'

I was immediately put at ease by his friendly greeting, and as he escorted me out of the station I was amazed to see parked at the edge of the pavement a dark box-like Black Maria, of the type used in my arrest. Alex laughed at my look of startled surprise.

'We'll bring you back the same way we brought you in!'

But this time I sat in the front of the van beside Alex and the driver, and the journey home was much longer than my trip in the same van three years previously had been. My parents had left the Cowcaddens and had gone to live in Bearsden, on the outskirts of Glasgow, and the police van crawled its way along the blacked-out streets, following the barely visible tram tracks for direction, The slow journey gave me just a little idea of what life must have been like in the winter in wartime Glasgow. Alex kept on chatting, giving me news of old friends. Do you remember so-and-so? Well, he was shot down and killed over France. And so-and-so? He died on a torpedoed merchant ship. And so-and so? Well, he's still around somewhere, as far as I know. And Sergeant Santangeli? He was badly wounded at El Alamein. And the realisation dawned on me that despite everything that had happened to me I had been one of the lucky ones.

My parents were overjoyed to see me alive and well, with mother crying tears of happiness every day and saying rosary after rosary of thanks for the return of her son. Despite their advancing years they had managed to keep the shop going, opening two days a week without help, paying the rent so that their sons could have something to come back to after war's end. They had nothing but praise for their neighbours, for despite their obvious Italian origin, made plain by their still-broken English, no harsh words had ever been addressed to them. Indeed, from what I could gather, everyone, neighbours and customers, seemed to have gone out of their way to be friendly and helpful. I was especially happy for my father. Given the indiscriminate nature of the early arrests, despite his age he too could well have finished up behind barbed wire. Not in the best of health, he might not have survived the trauma of the first weeks of internment and the dreadful conditions at Warth Mills, where, as I was to learn later, several old men in their seventies had died.

Slowly and tentatively I edged my way back into society. I had been allocated a job on a farm in Summerston, near Glasgow, and enjoyed the hard but healthy work there. The owner,

Tom McClymont, a dour honest Scot, treated me no differently than he did the rest of his workers, the bulk of whom were Land Army girls who didn't seem to care one jot what my background was as long as I did my work, and the months spent in that environment went a long way to easing the feeling of estrangement within me. Ironically, even on that farm there were times when I could almost feel myself back in Camp 43 on the St Lawrence river. Near to Glasgow, at Garelochhead, an Italian POW camp had been set up, and at times lorry-loads of prisoners were brought to the farm to help in the work. I would then take up my old role as interpreter, much to the delight of Tom McClymont, who was thereby relieved of the frustration of having to mime instructions to his Italian workers. I felt quite close to those POWs. It hadn't been so long since I had been in the position they were in, and I sympathised fully with them.

In the course of time I began to make contact with old friends and acquaintances, a process which I did not hurry and which I did not initiate. For obvious reasons I preferred them to make the first approach, and all who did seemed genuinely glad to see me. Not one harsh or insulting word did I hear, the one irritant being the constantly repeated enquiry as to how I had enjoyed my stay in Canada, as if I had been on holiday there. But then as I began to realise the nature of the sacrifices and the suffering everyone had undergone during those years of war, I could see that they might well consider me lucky in my experiences.'

Strangely enough, the war seemed to have brought about a change of attitude by the public towards the Italians in their midst. As the months and the years passed and as the restrictions on their movements eased, the ex-internees returned to their old places behind the counter of the cafés and fish and chip shops, once again to face the public across a shop counter. Remarkable though it may seem, old attitudes and prejudices had been transformed by the years of war. Where hostility and criticism might have been expected, the reverse was in fact the case.

Complete strangers, ex-soldiers who had fought in the Italian campaigns and who correctly assumed that the café or chip shop owner was Italian, would regale them with stories of their exploits in Italy and of the places they had visited. Of how they were treated as liberators, of the hospitality received from Italian families, of the food and wine they were offered by people who could ill afford to part with them, of the friendliness of the population in general and of the help given to British soldiers who had found themselves in danger behind the German lines. From time to time stories still appear in the press about the sacrifices made by some of the Italian populace in their efforts to shelter and help British servicemen. As these words are being written, in 2004, a story has just appeared in the *Mail on Sunday* written by a Lieutenant Alfred Burnford of the Royal Marines. The Lieutenant, now a retired doctor of 84, tells of how, wounded and starving and hiding behind enemy lines in the region of Monte Cassino he was given shelter by a young mother, Angelina Dimascio. She was a Glasgow-born Italian woman who had lived for a time in Scotland and now lived with her husband and baby in the town of Cardito in the shadow of Monte Cassino. Although the area was full of German SS, she hid and nursed the Lieutenant back to health until he was well enough to make his way back to the Allied lines. An informer betrayed the young woman to the Gestapo, and she and her entire family were executed.

There are many such stories told. As Barga is entered from the eastern side of the Serchio river, along Via Marconi an ironmonger's shop comes into view on the left hand side of a little piazza. Until the 1970s this used to be a little bar run by Luigi Clerici, a quiet and unassuming citizen of Barga. The only decoration on the walls was a framed commendation signed by General Alexander, British commander of the Army group who had fought in that sector of the Italian front. It commends Luigi Clerici for his bravery in hiding and assisting British soldiers to escape capture by the Germans over the period of a year. British soldiers who had escaped from POW camps at the time of Italy's capitulation were given refuge by him and then passed on to local partisan groups for assistance back to Allied lines. This was a highly dangerous procedure. In the autumn of 1943 to the spring of 1944, during the time of the German occupation of the area, 19 locals were executed by the Gestapo for giving assistance to the enemy. The copy of General Alexander's letter reproduced on the next page came into my possession as the result of a chance encounter with Michael Biagi, late of Glasgow, who now runs an estate agent's business in Barga, and who is a friend of the Clerici family.

Hugh Campbell of Glasgow, retired surgeon and once head of the departments of maxillo-facial surgery at the Southern General and Western Infirmaries, was an artilleryman in the Italian campaigns of 1943-45 and saw action at Monte Cassino and at the Salerno landings. At the end of the war in Italy he was assigned to a unit whose duty it was to discover the

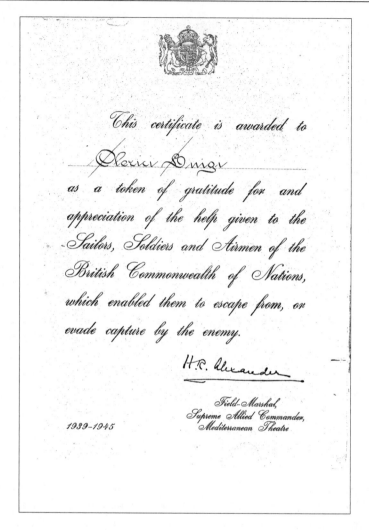

This certificate is awarded to

Alexander Dwyer

as a token of gratitude for and appreciation of the help given to the Sailors, Soldiers and Airmen of the British Commonwealth of Nations, which enabled them to escape from, or evade capture by the enemy.

H.R. Alexander

Field-Marshal,
Supreme Allied Commander,
Mediterranean Theatre

1939–1945

names of the many unidentified British soldiers killed in action. In the course of his duties he traveled the length and breadth of Italy, and was impressed by the help and friendliness of the Italian populace he came in contact with. He became enamoured of the country, studied Italian and during his distinguished career as a surgeon was for four years president of the Glasgow branch of the Dante Alighieri Society, an organization whose aim it is to bring about closer academic and cultural ties between the two countries. He tells the story of a doctor friend of his, Jake Mastarde, who later became an eminent eye surgeon in Glasgow. Mastarde was captured by the Germans in the region of Perugia with two other soldiers and was held prisoner in a trattoria. The trattoria had only one door, and this was locked and guarded by two soldiers pending arrival of transportation. Unknown to the Germans, however, the basement kitchen did have another door, which was accessible only by a very small food hoist from the restaurant area where the three prisoners were being held. The prisoners were jammed into the tiny hoist one at a time by the owner and sent down to the basement, where they made good their escape from the back door. Nothing is known of the fate of their benefactor.

Whatever the reason may have been, and it may simply have been that the British are magnanimous in victory, and realised that the hearts of the majority of the Italian people were never in the war against Britain, but that they were merely victims of circumstances outwith their control, the war seemed to have broadened minds and increased people's tolerance and understanding as far as the Italians in their midst were concerned.

Paradoxically, after all that had happened to them, the deportations to Canada and Australia, and the loss of life on the *Arandora Star*, for the first time in their lives many of these Italian ex-internees began to feel themselves welcome as part of the society into which they had returned to work and to live. Remarkable also is the fact that only a small handful of Italian families left Scotland to return to their homeland at war's end. The ones who did so were the ones who had lost fathers or husbands on the *Arandora Star* and no longer had a breadwinner to rely on. All those who had been interned on the Isle of Man went back to their shops and places of business to start again where they had so suddenly left off. Of the ones sent to Canada and Australia, a handful without any ties in Britain remained there to start a new life, but those with relations here all returned to their old places of business to begin dispensing fish and chips and ice-cream to the locals as though nothing had happened in the interim.

Most of the shops and businesses owned by the interned Italians had been repaired after the first night of vandalism and had somehow resumed trading. In most cases the doors had been kept open by the women of the family and by any aged male relative who had been fortunate enough to escape arrest and internment. The rationing of foodstuffs had meant that the opening hours of fish and chip shops were severely curtailed, but during these hours the wives and mothers did the same hard work their menfolk had once done. They went to the fish market to select fish, cleaned and gutted them, washed and chipped the potatoes, fried them and then served them up to the hungry customers.

In retrospect, it is remarkable that the families of the internees kept the businesses of their menfolk alive in this way. It was almost as if they had the collective belief, amounting to sure knowledge, that their husbands and sons would return home one day and that their lives could once more be lived as they had been in the happy and prosperous days before the war. During the dark days of the blitz, during the bombing of Greenock and Clydebank, at a time when one might have expected the anger and resentment of the locals to have reached breaking point and to have been directed at the Italians in their midst, there is no record, anecdotal or otherwise, of any Italian in Scotland, man or woman, having been verbally abused or molested physically in any way.

Indeed, those of the Italian community who lived through those times have nothing but praise for the behaviour of the Scottish populace towards them during the war years, and they all give voice to the fact that after the first few chaotic days of war, people in general behaved impeccably towards them, almost as if to make up for the wrongs some of the members of their families had suffered.

Xenophobia still existed in certain sections of the population of course, and still does. It is inherent in all societies and probably will never be bred out or eradicated. It stems from a dislike of the unfamiliar, from a fear of being swamped by strange cultures, from a dread of having one's religion and way of life changed by outside influences and from a desire inherent in all to maintain a familiar and comfortable status quo. In the early post-war years the focus of attention shifted from the likes of the Italians, the Poles and the Irish. These one-time immigrants had now become an accepted part of the settled community. The attention of the populace was now directed at the new immigrants who were arriving in vastly greater numbers than the early Italian settlers ever did. The Italians had arrived in their tens, the Asians and the Africans were now arriving in their tens of thousands. They were much easier to identify by their appearance than the Italians had been, for the colour of their skin was different and their manner of dress and lifestyle was different too. These newcomers took over whole sections of towns and cities as their enclaves and the xenophobes began to forget the 'Tallies'. They were now part of the familiar scenery. Other newcomers, readily indentifiable because of their dark skin, were now becoming the target of suspicion.

❖ 11 ❖

Modern Times

In the immediate post-war years, Italian immigration into Scotland grew quite rapidly. Many of the younger POWs with no family ties in Italy elected to remain here rather than return to their devastated homeland, and went to fill the labour shortages in the heavy industries and building trade. In the early 1950s an agreement was signed between the governments of Britain and Italy which allowed the entry of 2000 women to work in the textile industries, and these were soon followed by an equal amount of male workers who went to fill the manpower shortages in the construction industry and in the brickmaking factories of the Midlands. These workers were much sought after, for the Italians had the reputation of being hardworking and reliable.

In the same period Britain also recruited thousands of Italian workers for its overseas factories and industries. Several hundred miners and general labourers from the Garfagnana area of Tuscany were hired to work in the British-owned Yellowknife gold mines in the North-West territories of Canada, in an inhospitable environment where only the strongest of individuals could cope. The Garfagnana area, where Barga is located, was targeted because that district supplied the marble-mining industry of Cararra with much of its manpower. The skills of these men would have been invaluable in the development of the Yellowknife mines. The wages and conditions offered were so attractive that the vacancies could have been filled several times over, and the majority of the successful applicants remained in Yellowknife for the rest of their working days and raised families there.

Some of the POWs from the Gairloch camp met Scots-Italian girls, stayed on to marry and set up successful businesses here. A case in point is that of Albert Pacchini, founder of the Pacchini oil and wine importing company. Pacchini was made prisoner in the North African campaign and sent to the POW camp at Gairloch, where he remained for two years. After the war he was allowed to stay on in Scotland as a forestry worker, and met the daughter of a family who owned a fish and chip shop at Temple Bridge at Anniesland. They married and he set up a little oil and wine importing business in Gibson Street, which was to expand rapidly over the years and is now one of the biggest of its kind in Scotland.

The Duke of Argyll, who had commanded a unit in Italy during the war, had formed a great liking for the country, and from the time of the capitulation of Italy had taken as his personal batman an Italian from Barga, a POW captured by the British at the Sicily landings. After the war, this soldier came to Scotland as a forestry worker, and was given permission to open a café in Inveraray, a town which formed part of the Duke's extensive estates. He made a fortune there, since his was the only planning permission granted in Inveraray for such a use. In the early 1950s, given the shortage of local labour, the Duke brought over several hundred forestry workers from the Lucca–Barga region to work on his estates, and many of them were allowed to remain here after their contract period had elapsed. They followed in the footsteps of their predecessors, sought work in cafes and restaurants and then, having learned the trade and saved a little money, set themselves up in places of their own. The Italian population in the UK grew steadily from 38,000 in 1951 to 109,000 in 1971, and in the year 2000 Italian consular sources give the number of persons bearing Italian passports in Britain as 156,776, with 10,895 of these in Scotland.

Glasgow in the post-war years had started on a massive and comprehensive programme of city redevelopment. The old slum areas, the Gorbals, the Cowcaddens, the Anderston district and others were being razed to the ground and a new modern city was arising where the old grimy tenements had once stood. Motor roads and ring roads now criss-crossed Glasgow, and in the space of a few years a handsome modern city had arisen from the rubble of the old. As the old buildings and districts vanished, so did the old unpretentious and often dingy cafes and fish and chip shops and other relics of the pre-war years which once catered for the public in these districts. To many of the shop owners in the redevelopment areas of the city, the loss of their business through compulsory purchase was a blessing in disguise, and not the end of everything they had worked for as originally had been feared. The owners of these old shops were awarded generous compensation by the local authority for the loss of their business, and for the first time in their lives many of them had at their disposal substantial sums to invest in new and modern premises.

The redevelopment of Glasgow had another effect. With the demolition of the old slum tenements and the factories which surrounded them, new dormitory towns were built on the outskirts of the city, and workers were now travelling to their place of work, which often were relocated in one of the new industrial estates. No longer did the workers go to their factories or offices with a lunch box or a humble 'piece' made up at home, nor did they now live two minutes walk or a penny tram tide away from their tenement flats. This gave rise to the need for catering outlets in both places, the dormitory towns and the industrial estates, and in these areas the capital acquired by the old fish and chip shop and café owners was put to the opening of catering establishments in keeping with the needs of a new and modern city, and infinitely more profitable than their old shops had ever been.

The Scots had now become much more discerning and sophisticated in their tastes. The coming of the package holiday had introduced them to the greater variety offered by European resorts, and to cater for these new expectations the humble carry-out fish and chip shops slowly evolved into the modern neon-lit fast food takeaways now to be found in their dozens in every neighbourhood. The old fashioned corner cafés too had been bull-dozed out of existence, and had been reborn as state-of-the-art modern coffee bars and caféterias in the new glass and steel buildings appearing in the city.

For those Glaswegians whose tastes leaned to Italian food rather than to Chinese or Indian dishes, pizzerias and trattorias were now appearing on the scene. The first Italian trattoria-style eating place in Glasgow was the Canasta in Parliamentary Road, which opened in the late 1950s by the side of the well-known San Remo chip shop and was owned by the same family. This type of eating place with its informal and homely Italian atmosphere, serving good and reasonably priced food, came as a novelty to the Glasgow public, and a table had to be booked days in advance. The Canasta was followed in rapid succession by the Sorrento in Buchanan Street, which not only supplied excellent Italian food but soothed the customers with the music from a strolling guitar player, possessed of a repertoire of all the favourite Italian songs. The Vesuvius restaurant in St Vincent Street at George Square followed soon after, and the city centre was beginning to take on a distinctly Italian atmosphere. Then another trend was set by the opening of La Buca Pizzeria in Hope Street. The word 'pizza' was relatively unknown to Glasgwegians, but La Buca, opened by a young Roman, Enzo De Caris, started a fashion in eating which has culminated in the Neapolitan pizza becoming as popular here as it is in its homeland on the bay of Naples, if not more so. There is hardly a neighbourhood in Glasgow or Edinburgh now which does not have in it a pizzeria or Italian restaurant, many of which are of exceptional quality.

Then in the 1960s a young Neapolitan with drive and ambition arrived in Glasgow, and in the space of a few years had opened a chain of spaghetti houses in the city centre which gave a further dimension to the choice available to Glasgow diners. Mario Romano came to Glasgow from Naples with well developed commercial ideas and a burning desire to become a mini-Charles Forte. Intelligent, and above all street-wise, he worked for a spell in a fish and chip shop in Maryhill Road until a command of English and knowledge of the environment had been acquired, then proceeded on a meteor-like career. A run-down cafeteria in Bath Street at West Nile Street was acquired and became the trattoria O Sole Mio. Some months later, following the spectacular success of that establishment, Mario's Spaghetti House appeared beside the entrance of the Regal Cinema in Sauchiehall Street, then in rapid succession the Ambassador in Blytheswood Square and the Ariosto at the bottom of West Nile Street went to swell his empire, after which the Country Club Hotel at Strathblane was added to his list. Then, at the time of the Glasgow Garden Festival in the late eighties, Romano added a jewel to his crown. In the early years of the twentieth century a pedestrian tunnel ran under the Clyde from Lancefield Quay on the north side to Springfield Quay on the south. A circular structure called the Rotunda housed the ventilating pumps for this passageway, and had lain derelict since the closure of the tunnel in the early 1930s. The Glasgow exhibition centre had been built just a short distance away. Seizing the opportunity, Mario acquired the derelict Rotunda, converted it into a popular trattoria with a first class restaurant on the upper floors, then obtained a gaming license for its use as a gambling casino.

The eating habits of the Glaswegians had changed. Firstly the Cypriot Stakis with his chain of steak houses, and now Mario Romano with his trattorias and spaghetti houses had given the populace a variety of eating places previously unknown to them. No longer did cinema or theatre-goers partake simply of a modest fish tea before a visit to the local cinema or city centre theatre. They now had a choice of far more exotic dishes than just a fish supper or its companion, a pie and chips, before sitting down to watch Marilyn Monroe on the cinemascope screen.

The money that was now to be made in catering, and the freedom of movement afforded by the new European common market, attracted Italian entrepreneurs to Glasgow in their scores. These were no longer the semi-literate immigrants of 80 or more years ago. They were astute and sophisticated businessmen with money to invest and with the expertise to invest it well, and this they did, in ever more opulent coffee bars, restaurants and hotels. The descendants of the old immigrants had progressed too. The Sarti brothers started their own chain of attractive restaurants, and the Conettas, the Giovanazzis, the Di Ciaccas, the Equis and the Crollas, all of them now second and third generation Italians, were also opening new takeaways, pizzerias and restaurants of high quality. In Edinburgh the firm of Valvona and Crolla began to set new standards in the field of Italian delicatessen, and now offers fine foods and wines from around the world. It has a popular restaurant and a tasting and demonstration room which sometimes is used as a Fringe venue, and recently presented the stage version of *Captain Corelli's Mandolin*.

By the end of the twentieth century, only a handful of the original immigrants to Scotland were still alive. The vast majority of the Scots-Italians were now all second or third generation Italians. Their immigrant grandfathers and fathers of the early twentieth century had now mostly passed away or were long retired, and new generations with new values had taken their place. The memory of the war and of the internment of their fathers and grandfathers had long faded away. Many of the new generations had taken to the professions, to the arts and to the media. Sir Eduardo Paolozzi and Alberto Morrocco became prominent on the post-war arts scene, as did Jack Coia the architect. Tom Conti and Peter Capaldi are stars of the stage and screen; Marcella Evaristi is a playwright and popular newspaper columnist, Terri Colpi of Milngavie is a noted writer, whose *Italians Forward*, a pictorial history of Italian immigration to Britain, has received the accolade of the Scottish Arts Council. Anne Marie Di Mambro is a prolific scriptwriter for Scottish Television, and her play 'Tally Blood', which deals with the tragedy that befalls a Scots-Italian family during the war, has been acclaimed by the critics and has been doing the rounds of Scottish theatres for the last ten years. Richard Demarco, a co-founder of the Traverse Theatre and the name behind a string of art galleries, is a giant in the world of the theatre and the visual arts. In the realm of the law, Joe Beltrami, of Swiss-Italian origin, for decades was the most sought-after criminal lawyer in Scotland, whilst Frank Pieri, son of one of the Pieri brothers Ralph, has had a spectacular career in law, first with his own law firm, then as an advocate, and now has been appointed Sheriff.

The ceremony took place in the Sheriff Court Buildings in Hamilton and was presided over by the Sheriff Principal John C. McInnes QC. His speech included the following little gem, which although it has nothing to do with the Scots-Italians is worthy of inclusion here. He is referring to the career of one of Frank Pieri's colleagues who has also been elevated to the rank of Sheriff:

'Sheriff Smith has a baccalaureate in philosophy from Rome. Sheriff, you will find that there are many philosophers among those who appear in front of you in court. Their concepts may differ from yours in some respects—concepts such as right and wrong and duty, but I know that you will be able to address their errors in such a way as to increase their understanding.'

To return to the Scots-Italians. Rigo Capanni, now retired and living with his wife Anne in Bishopbriggs, did much of his studying for his university degree in between preparing and serving fish and chips in his father's shop in Royston Road. He went on to become principal maths teacher in Holyrood, and has compiled six books on mathematics which were used until recently as textbooks in Scottish schools.

Daniela Nardini, granddaughter of one of the original Nardinis of Largs, is now a famous actress and appears regularly on stage and screen. She is the winner of a BAFTA award for her work in the BBC production *This Life*. Dario Franchitti is one of today's most successful racing drivers and Michael Biagi of Edinburgh, grandson of an immigrant from Barga, is making a name for himself as a photographer with work which rivals that of his great Italian-American predecessor of a generation ago, Frank Capa. The popular artist Jack Vettriano was born Jack Hoggan in Fife. However, he is Scots-Italian on his mother's side, and early in his career adopted the name of his maternal grandfather, who was a strong influence on him as a young boy.

In the field of football too, the names of many Scots-Italians are household words. In the immediate post-war years Freddie Renucci, the son of the Kelvindale baker Renucci, made a name for himself as goalkeeper for Partick Thistle, and Lou Macari, whose parents ran an ice-cream shop on the promenade at Largs, became nationally famous as a player for Glasgow Celtic and later for Manchester United. At this same time Peter Marinello was scoring goals for Arsenal and Joe Tortolano was a great favourite of the Hibs fans. The skills of Paul Di Ciacomo were roundly applauded by the followers of Kilmarnock and the Celtic goalposts were very successfully defended for several seasons by Rolando Ugolini of Glasgow. The names of Paolo Di Canio, who was once named Scottish footballer of the year and who played for Celtic for a spell, and those of Lorenzo Amoruso, one-time captain of Rangers, and Gennaro Gattuso, also of Rangers, perhaps should not be included here, since they were not the sons of immigrants and took the high road purely for short-term financial reasons. Together with Ivano and Dario Bonetti, erstwhile managers of Dundee, they could be likened to the Scottish soldier mercenaries who sold their services to the Italian city states all those centuries ago. They have made as big an impact on Scottish football as their Scottish soldier counterparts made in the wars in Italy in the fourteenth century.

Barga, the little hilltop Tuscan town whose sons and daughters long ago took the high road and started it all, has changed with the times. The grinding poverty which once forced its sons to seek a life in other lands no longer exists, and the poor crofts which once dotted the neighbouring hills are no longer there. In their place there now stand magnificent villas built by the wealthy of Europe. Barga, now rich and prosperous, has become a Mecca for those who seek the flavour of Tuscany and posters of the town in all its beauty can be seen in the travel agencies of Europe. So internationally known has it become that 'Il Ciocco', a luxury hotel built a few kilometres away, on a site where a crofting family once lived, is used by internationally renowned football teams as a summer training centre, and has been occupied on several occasions by Glasgow Rangers and visiting Russian teams.

The chestnut forest which surrounded Bacchionero has disappeared and the bulldozers will soon be at work where the church once stood, preparing the site for a luxury hotel and leisure centre. The millhouse known as Carletti, once a hive of activity at harvest times and deserted since the Santi family emigrated to France 40 years ago, still stands derelict over the rushing stream, and has just been sold to an Englishman for 400,000 Euros. It will cost him another million to make it habitable.

As part of an ongoing cultural collaboration with the Italian province of Lucca, Glasgow City Council recently agreed to host an exhibition of Italian painting in the Mitchell Library under the title 'This Enchanted Land'. This was the name given by the poet Shelley to the Serchio valley and the towns which dot the meandering path of the river as it flows through this part of Tuscany. The theme of the exhibition was the variety of landscapes in the region as seen through the eyes of British and Italian painters from the middle of the nineteenth century to the present day. The event highlighted the many links, both cultural and commercial, that exist between Scotland and Tuscany and in particular between Glasgow and Barga. Glasgow City Councillor Alex Mosson, who originally proposed the exhibition, received the wholehearted collaboration of the Mayor of Barga, who is the son of Bruno Sereni, the founder of the local newspaper. The exhibition was dominated by the works of John Bellany, the Scottish artist who has lived in Barga for some years and who has painted many paintings of the town and the surrounding countryside.

An enchanted land it is indeed, this part of Tuscany, with its rolling hills and magnificent vistas of the Apuan Alps, and it is no wonder that the descendants of those who came away from it to seek their bread in other lands are drawn back time and time again to the birthplace of their ancestors. Emigrants left here for the four corners of the world. There are Barghigiani in America, they are to be found in Canada, Australia and New Zealand, in France, Germany and Belgium, in Switzerland and in parts of England, but above all they came to Scotland. They took the high road in their hundreds to Inverness, to Glasgow, to Edinburgh, to Aberdeen, to Dumfries, to Largs, Ayr, Troon and Prestwick, to Auchinleck and Mauchline, to Newmills and to Aberdeen and Dundee. Take a walk through the narrow cobbled streets of the old centre of Barga, stop at any bar or restaurant, pause to take in the magnificent views from the square in front of the old Cathedral, and everywhere you will hear English spoken, almost always with a Scottish accent. One wonders how this little hilltop town of no more than a few thousand inhabitants could have sent so many of its sons to distant lands, and the wonder is increased when one thinks that so many of them came to Glasgow and the West of Scotland.

Barga has its own newspaper, *Il Giornale di Barga*, founded in the late forties by the late Bruno Sereni, a Barghigiano whose eventful life merits a book in itself. A soldier in the First World War and a vocal critic of fascism, he was exiled because of his political views, first to America and then to Glasgow, where he worked for two years, 1931 and 1932, in the Savoy fish and chip shop. He fought in the International Brigade against Franco and at the end of that war was forced to take refuge in France. He was given an amnesty by the fascists and returned to Italy, but came within a whisker of being executed by the Germans during their occupation of Barga during the war. He was denounced to the Gestapo as a communist by a local fascist official and locked up in the local prison together with two others. His companions were put to death, but he was saved by the rapid advance of the Allied armies in that sector. The 8th Indian division of the British 5th army group had made a lightning advance north along the line of the Serchio valley and forced the Nazis to retreat hurriedly from Barga on the eve of Sereni's scheduled execution. His newspaper, the *Giornale di Barga*, which deals with affairs of local interest, is sold by subscription only, and is mailed each month to the four corners of the world.

A tradition has been formed that on arrival in Barga, the returning pilgrim makes a visit to the tiny office of the paper in Via Di Mezzo, there to have his name inserted as a visitor in the next edition. In years gone by this tradition included the visitor placing a banknote from his country of origin under the glass top of Bruno Sereni's desk, and his desk is there, still in use, with banknotes from practically every country in the world spread out under the glass top. For decades Bruno Sereni was always to be found behind this desk to welcome visitors, especially those from Glasgow, with whom he had a special rapport because of the two years he had spent there. He spoke a little English, with a thick Scottish–Italian accent, and liked to tell with a great deal of relish of how his first words learned in that language were 'Big fight in shop', which he uttered in the Northern Police Station in Maitland Street on the numerous occasions when sent there for police assistance by Francesco Pieri, the owner of the Savoy fish and chip shop where he worked. Because of the number of drunks who sought out fish and chip shops after pub closing-time, disturbances were a frequent occurrence in them, and the Savoy was particularly vulnerable.

This is the list of overseas visitors to Barga for the month of September, with their place of origin as listed in the *Giornale di Barga*:

From The USA
From Chicago Illinois: Mr Aldo Giuntini with Semantha Gesser
From Richmond Virginia: Richard Tonacci with his wife
    Antonia
From Bayville NJ: Sig. Arrighi with his family
From Tinton Falls NJ: Giulia Stevens and family
From Rutherford N J: Eduardo Gonella with his wife Desi
From Park Way Illinois: Luccero Luccherini
From Richmond Virginia: Maria Ghiloni with her friend
    Melissa Chirico

From Australia
From Adelaide: Mr and Mrs Biagi
From Melbourne: Domenica Tognazzi

From Gt. Britain
From Kirkintilloch Scotland: Mr and Mrs Ghiloni
From Glasgow Scotland: Mr Liano Luccherini with his wife
    Patricia and son Marco
From Paisley Scotland: Alberta Tonacci Stevens
From Saltcoats Scotland: Francesco and Anna Maria Cecchini
From Carlisle England: Alberto Dianda with his wife Rosita

From Glasgow Scotland: Mr and Mrs Peter and Olga Marchetti

From Glasgow Scotland: Miranda and Bruno Togneri

From Dundee Scotland: Lorenzo Dello Sterpaio with his wife
    Dorothy

From Saltcoats Scotland: Grazia Biagi with her husband Willie
    Gibson

From Paisley Scotland: Dante and Teresa Toti

From Dumfries, Scotland: Mr and Mrs Lorenzo Rinaldi

From Newmills Scotland: Luigi and Verena Nardini

From Dumfries Scotland: Delia Moscardini with husband Cliff
    Montgomery

From Sutton England: Mrs Anna Maria McPherson

From Glasgow Scotland: Mr and Mrs Stefano and Maria Biagi

From Canada Toronto: Adriano and Pina Funai

From Kent England: Mary Cecchini with husband Alan Gibbons

From Paisley Scotland: Mr Giuntini with wife Joyce

From Largs Scotland: Michael and Lynne Donnelly with Ted
    and Emma Keegan

From Paisley Scotland: Ricardo Cardosi with his wife Colette

From Troon Scotland: Mr Dorando Badiali

From Ayr Scotland: Mr Piero Vanucci and his son Gianpiero

From Kirkton England: Lina Munroe with daughter Laura

From Europe

From Zurich Switzerland: Mr and Mrs Enrico and Filomena
    Marchetti

From Brussels Belgium: Mrs Maria Gonella

From Geneva Switzerland: Mr Franco Diversi

Each entry is accompanied by a brief history of the persons concerned.

Some of the couples listed are 'mixed', that is to say that one or other of them are Scottish. Although the old days when 'mixed' marriages between Italian and Scot were almost unheard of and actively discouraged are now gone, there is still a strong tendency for Italians to marry into other Italian families. Some of the older generation remain nostalgic for the old days when arranged marriages were a common occurrence, and marriage to a non-Italian was regarded as anathema, but no longer does a tinge of ostracism intrude into families when Italian marries Scot or Scot marries Italian, and it is probably only among the old that such considerations are even thought of.

However, fifty years ago such marriages could bring about deep and sometimes irreconcilable divisions in Italian families. Pages could be filled with examples of families torn apart because someone had followed the dictates of the heart and married 'una Scozzese'.

Now Barga is intensely proud of its Scottish connection, and the recent visit of the Lady Provost of Edinburgh which followed the recent visit of her Glasgow counterpart Alex Mosson was recorded in the *Giornale di Barga* by the Mayor Umberto Sereni, son of the founder Bruno, with these words: 'This is a day which will go down in the history of Barga, because it bears witness to the proud fact that Barga is the most Scottish of all Italian towns.'

There is now no single focal point for the Italians of Scotland to meet. The Casa D'Italia closed down in 1985, for there was no longer the need or the desire for it. Italians had now become socially acceptable and were now being admitted to clubs whose doors had hitherto been closed to them. They no longer felt the need for their own exclusive venue, which by its very nature as an 'Italian' club would have been open to all Italians, no matter what their social or financial standing. The Scots-Italians of the modern era do not by any manner of means share the same financial or social background or patterns of behaviour, and tend to seek out clubs on the basis of financial and social worth, rather than ethnic background. Where in pre-war days the young Italians who wanted to play golf had to confine themselves to the municipal courses, there is scarcely a golf club of any renown in Scotland which does not have its quota of Italian names as members. Many of the younger generation no longer speak Italian, but this does not blunt their pride in an Italian heritage and their love of things Italian: music, food and fast cars. It has to be said, however, that there is a tendency in some of the modern generation to lose the true heritage of things Italian in a flood of Hollywood Martin Scorsese Mafia-type movies, to the detriment of the values of Dante, Michelangelo, Danilo Dolci and Umberto Eco.

These values, however are kept alive by the activities of the Dante Alighieri Society, an association which has as its purpose the spreading and appreciation of the language and the culture of Italy. Already in existence in countries throughout the world since the beginning of the twentieth century, the Scottish branch of the Society was opened in Edinburgh in 1952, and now has branches in five other Scottish centres: Glasgow, Falkirk, Dundee, Lanark and Aberdeen. The Glasgow branch has had a number of eminent office bearers since its foundation. These have included Jack Coia the architect, Lord Provost Thomas Kerr and Hugh Campbell, the eminent Glasgow facial surgeon, who for many years served on the committee and then himself became president. The Dante Alighieri Society has done much to make the language and culture of Italy known to the Scots through its programmes of Italian drama and music and talks by academics, musicians, artists, politicians and social workers. Amongst these was Danilo Dolci, who in 1963 addressed the Society with a talk on the problems of Sicily and its Mafia.

There are still gatherings and dances where the flavour and music of an older Italy are kept alive, and the Laziale club, which meets in St Thomas' church hall in Riddrie every month or so in the winter, is in the forefront of these. The Laziale club was the brainchild of an Italian priest, Padre Zorza, whose concept of a social evening for like-minded Italians and their Scottish friends was seized upon and developed by three friends, Marcello Di Tano, a retired hairdresser, his brother in law Alberto Pacitti and the late John Romano (no relation to the catering entrepreneur) both retired teachers. The three began to organise monthly Italian dances in St Thomas' church hall, and these became an instant success. On the death of Romano, Marcello, with the help of his wife Lucy, kept the club going and it became one of the most eagerly awaited and well-attended occasions in the older Italians' social calendar. The music at these dances was originally provided by a little group of part-time musicians, 'I Paesani', led by Peter Vezza the hairdresser. By the use of mandolin, guitar and accordion, the group provided a music which, although not of the highest professional standard, had a unique and nostalgic Italian quality which no one else could ever reproduce. Tragically, two years ago Lucy Di Tano passed away, but Marcello, now helped by his son Armando, an electronics engineer from Edinburgh, carries the tradition on, and the Laziale club nights are eagerly awaited by the Italians and their Scottish friends. I Paesani are long gone, and the music is now provided by a professional husband and wife team, Angela and Paolo, who also create a unique Italian sound and can also cater for those of more modern musical tastes. The guests are in the main elderly, but there are hopeful signs that some of the younger generation are being attracted to these occasions so evocative of their Italian heritage.

Nearly sixty years ago an idea born in the back-shop of the Risi Brothers Italian Grocers in Stockwell Street gave rise to another institution which now helps to keep the younger generation of Scots-Italians together. That institution, which brought about the most eagerly awaited Italian social evening of the year, is the Scots-Italian Golfing Society, or Club, as they call themselves. The S.I.G.S. was founded 57 years ago and was the brainchild of Albert Risi, his brother Ernie, and two keen Glasgow golfers, Dom Valerio and Silvio Rinaldi. In those days very few Italians were members of private golf clubs. Firstly there was religious factor; many clubs would not accept Catholics as members, and many would not accept Italians, so any budding young Italian golfer, even if he had the money to join a club, had two reasons for being blackballed. Moreover, very few in those days could afford the financial outlay involved in joining a private club, so the ones who played golf, and the game was becoming ever more popular among the young Italians, had no other choice but to play on the Glasgow municipal courses. The idea of forming an Italian Golfing Society was developed by the three friends and soon the new organisation attracted a considerable number of members. Two of the original founders, Ernie Risi and Silvio Rinaldi passed away, but Albert kept the club going, and their place was taken by Peter Coia and Virgil Franchetti. The group continued to meet on a regular basis at municipal courses, and the matches would be followed by a get-together and a meal at some restaurant or other.

The Jewish community in Glasgow faced the same problem of discrimination in those days. Many clubs were closed to them, but since they were far greater in number than the Italians and some were very wealthy, they bypassed the problem by buying their own golf course at Bonnyton.

Now, fifty and more years on, the scene has altered considerably. The Italians are no longer second-class citizens, they are as affluent as any, to say the least of it, and discrimination no longer exists in clubs, at least overtly, so practically every golf club in the West of Scotland now has its little group of Italian members, many of whom belong to the S.I.G.S. The Society meets on a monthly basis, when they become a visiting party at some chosen golf course, and the hallowed turf of the likes of Gleneagles, Turnberry, Prestwick and St Andrews has had many a divot taken by its members. A far cry indeed from the games played on Glasgow municipal courses such as Littlehill, Ruchill, Linn Park and Deaconsbank a half century ago. The players no longer seek out some nearby modest restaurant as their nineteenth hole. The dining room and bar of the host club do record business on the occasion of their visits, and the array of Ferraris and Mercedes in the car park bears mute witness to the changed status of what were once the self-styled 'poveri Italiani'. The Society now owns a luxurious apartment in Marbella which the members can use in turn if they so wish, and thus play golf in the sun all year round if the fancy takes them. Once a year the Society holds its Ladies and Prizegiving night in a city centre hotel. The occasion is a glamorous and spectacular success, and tickets are at a premium for what has become a showpiece function for the Scot-Italians of the Glasgow-Edinburgh corridor.

To the modern generation of Scots the 'Tallies' are now no longer associated only with fish and chips and ice-cream, as they were in days gone by, but are accepted as being an integral part of Scottish society and are recognised as having contributed much to the culture and attractions of Glasgow. As an embodiment of this is the Italian Centre by the side of the municipal buildings at George Square, an Italian-style shopping complex. The architecture, the Armani and Versace shops, the bars, the coffee houses and the general ambience are no different from those to be found in Milan or Turin. Perhaps, however, a young 18-year-old Scots-Italian girl from East Kilbride epitomises the prominent role that those of Italian descent now play in Scottish society. Nicola Benedetti had the honour of playing the violin at the opening of the new Scottish Parliament building in Edinburgh.

The old 'Tallies' of 100 years ago, who took the high road to Scotland and who pushed their barrel-organs and ice-cream carts through the streets of Scottish towns and cities, could never have dreamed of these developments. They and those who followed their footsteps have had, in their own way, as much impact on Scotland as did their forebears who marched here in the Roman legions of 2000 years ago.